FUNDAMENTAL HARMONY

by

Hugo Norden, D.Mus.

Professor of Music Theory

SCHOOL OF FINE AND APPLIED ARTS
BOSTON UNIVERSITY

CRESCENDO PUBLISHING COMPANY

BOSTON

Standard Book Number 87597-029-X
Library of Congress Card Number 73-123576
Printed in the United States of America
Copyright © 1971 by Crescendo Publishing Company
All Rights Reserved

TO GEORGE A. BRAMBILLA

CONTENTS

FOREWORD

Over the years the study of Harmony has accumulated and subsequently has become encumbered with a considerable number of minutiae in the form of rules, restrictions and clichés that have but little relevance to the creative problems confronting the composer of today. These venerable academic teachings, many of which bear only a distant relationship to the actual music of any period, can cause the conscientious student to be burdened with something akin to the sin of supererogation, often hindering rather than stimulating creative enterprise. Yet, they do represent well certain facets of a neatly packaged combinatorial system which is the wellspring of all musical composition, regardless of style or period.

Because of these considerations a genuinely comprehensive treatise on Harmony in the traditional sense becomes self-defeating. This is so because no matter how many rules and specific exceptions with supporting illustrations are provided, one need not look far in the music of the great masters to encounter ingenious and artistically valid harmonizations that defy these long honored teachings.

Therefore, in keeping with the artistically venturesome spirit of the present day it seems more relevant to look at Harmony in its relationship first to actual practical music and, secondly, to the broad creative availabilities of this all-encompassing and pregnant combinatorial system. Thus, the present volume is intended more to serve as a sort of "launching pad" whereby the young composer will give wings to his musical ideas rather than to provide him with a catechism of outdated and all too often inhibiting theories. Thus, some matters are touched upon only lightly while still others are presented in a sequence that knowledgeable connoisseurs of Harmony textbooks may not normally expect.

This book is meant merely to serve as a beginning for the inquisitive and questioning student. The music of the masters is his source of enlightenment. To this end, and again for a beginning, he is urged to take as his constant companion during these studies Johann Sebastian Bach's 371 Four-Part Chorales. Herein is to be found one of the most technically sophisticated and artistically superlative exercises in harmonic organization of all time up to the present.

Boston, Massachusetts

Hugo Norden

July 1, 1970

ABBREVIATIONS

Concerning intervals and chords:

M major
m minor
P perfect
d diminished
A augmented

Concerning keys:

Major key indicated by capital letter; as G: being G major.
Minor key indicated by lower case letter; as g: being G minor.

Concerning discords:

ant. anticipation
ap. appoggiatura
aux. auxiliary-note
ech. échappée
p.n. passing-note
r. retardation
s. suspension

INTRODUCTION

THE COMBINATORIAL SYSTEM

1. Music is a combinatorial art. The raw material that is available for artistic combination vertically into chords and sequentially into melodic lines consists of twelve notes. These can be seen most easily from their arrangement on the keyboard as it is employed on the piano and organ:

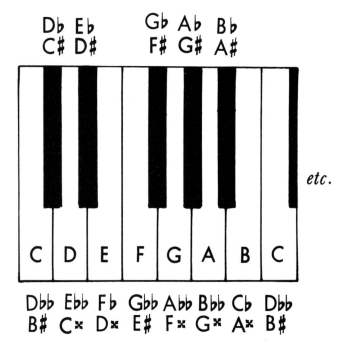

On the staff these twelve notes appear in the treble clef as follows,

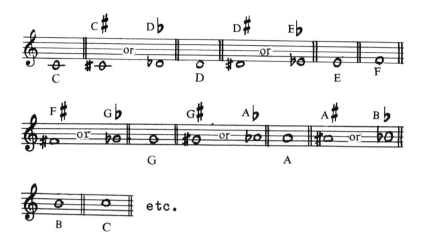

and with the bass clef:

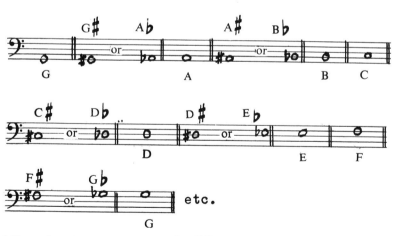

When the same note appears in different ways as, for instance, C-sharp and D-flat, this is referred to as *enharmonic* notation.

2. Sharps (♯), flats (♭) and naturals (♮) before a note are generally referred to as *accidentals*. The system of accidentals also includes the double-sharp (𝄪) and double-flat (♭♭) which can be applied to any white note on the keyboard that is adjacent to a black note, either above or below it. For instance,

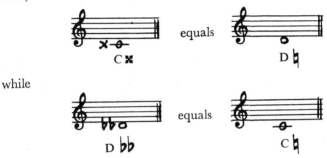

while

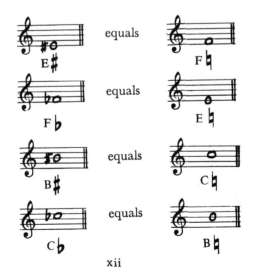

Double-sharps are not applied to B or E, nor double-flats to C or F as B - C and E - F are adjacent notes. However, a sharp or flat makes the following white note enharmonic equivalents available:

xii

3. From any note, for example C, to the same note at its next higher or lower recurrence the interval (that is, the distance between any two notes) is called an *octave* (8ve) for the obvious reason that these two notes encompass eight lines and spaces on the staff.

*Added lines above or below the staff are called *leger lines*.

Thus, the interval between any two adjacent notes is 1/12 of an 8ve, regardless of any enharmonic notation. From this simple arithmetical fact the following system of intervals exists:

1/12 of an 8ve = Minor 2nd and its enharmonics

2/12 of an 8ve = Major 2nd and its enharmonics

3/12 of an 8ve = Minor 3rd and its enharmonics

4/12 of an 8ve = Major 3rd and its enharmonics

5/12 of an 8ve = Perfect 4th and its enharmonics

6/12 of an 8ve = Augmented 4th and Diminished 5th

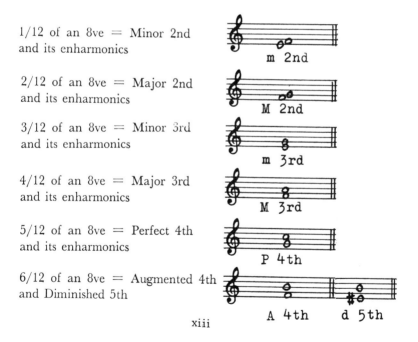

7/12 of an 8ve = Perfect 5th
and its enharmonics

8/12 of an 8ve = Minor 6th
and its enharmonics

9/12 of an 8ve = Major 6th
and its enharmonics

10/12 of an 8ve = Minor 7th
and its enharmonics

11/12 of an 8ve = Major 7th
and its enharmonics

12/12 of an 8ve = 8ve
and its enharmonics

The same note being sounded at once by two voices or instruments is called either *unison* or *prime*.

4. The unison, 4th, 5th and 8ve are either *perfect* or *imperfect* while the 2nd, 3rd, 6th and 7th are *major* or *minor*. However, accidentals make available the following identification substitutions within the 12/12 fractionization of the 8ve:

    (1) *Perfect* and *minor* intervals become *diminished* when they are reduced by 1/12 of an 8ve either by raising the lower note or by lowering the upper note.

(2) *Perfect* and *major* intervals become *augmented* when they are expanded by 1/12 of an 8ve either by lowering the lower note or by raising the upper note.

P 5th   A 5th   M 6th   A 6th

(3) *Minor* intervals become *major* when they are expanded by 1/12 of an 8ve either by lowering the lower note or by raising the upper note.

m 3rd   M 3rd

(4) *Major* intervals become *minor* when they are reduced by 1/12 of an 8ve either by raising the lower note or by lowering the upper note.

M 7th   m 7th

5. Any interval may be expanded by one or more 8ves to form a so-called *compound* interval. For instance, a major 3rd

M 3rd

expanded by an 8ve becomes a major 10th,

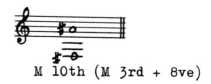

M 10th (M 3rd + 8ve)

and when expanded by two 8ves becomes a major 17th.

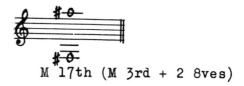

M 17th (M 3rd + 2 8ves)

An interval remains the same whether it is written on one staff or on two; that is to say, the major 10th shown above could be written thus:

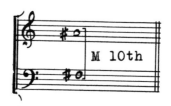

M 10th

6. These intervals provide the material from which are built the chords used in Harmony. Four types of three-note chords called *triads* constitute the basic harmonic equipment for the writing of music.

Major Triad: Minor Triad:

Diminished Triad: Augmented Triad:

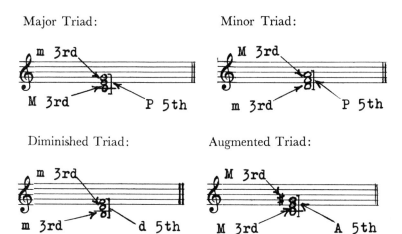

The three notes of the triad, beginning with the lowest, are spoken of as *root*, *third* (3rd) and *fifth* (5th).

7. The distribution of the four kinds of triads within the major and minor keys is as shown below, being identified by the Roman numeral corresponding to the scale degree on which the root occurs. They are further identified by the name given below each Roman numeral.

Major Key:

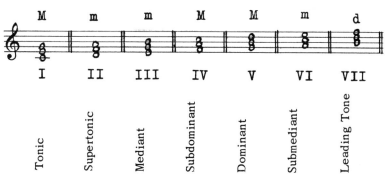

Minor Key:

m	d	A	m	M	M	d
I	II	III	IV	V	VI	VII
Tonic	Supertonic	Mediant	Subdominant	Dominant	Submediant	Leading Tone

This entire triadic system prevails in every major and minor key.

8. The preceding material is concerned chiefly with vertical combinations in terms of triads, although the various intervals function melodically as well. The major-minor harmonic system is based mainly upon two scales, the *major* and the *minor,* the latter having three forms. These can be shown without further explanation thus.

Major Scale:

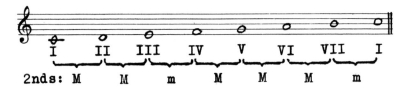

2nds: M   M   m   M   M   M   m

Minor Scale (beginning on the 6th degree of the major scale):
   (1) Natural form:

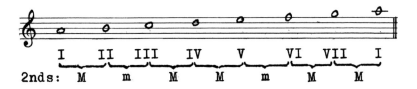

2nds: M   m   M   M   m   M   M

xviii

(2) Harmonic form:

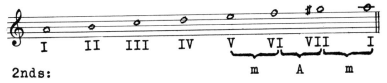

I	II	III	IV	V	VI	VII	I

2nds: m   A   m

(3) Melodic form:

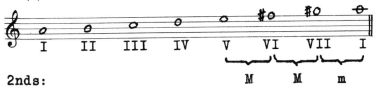

I	II	III	IV	V	VI	VII	I

2nds: M   M   m

The natural minor scale is generally used for purposes of descending in relation to the ascending melodic form as shown above.

9. A major scale and the minor scale the I of which is a minor 3rd below that of the major scale are said to be *relative,* and share the same key signature. A major or minor scale can begin on any of the twelve points within the octave as given in paragraph 1. However, because of unavoidable excessive notational complexity major scales are not normally constructed with G-sharp or A-sharp as I, nor are minor scales constructed with D-flat or G-flat as I.

10. This all too brief and sketchy introduction about the combinatorial system provides minimal background for proceeding with the study of Harmony. The student is urged to pursue these matters further in more comprehensive texts on elementary music theory and also in acoustics.

CHAPTER I

BASIC PROGRESSION PRINCIPLES

1. A *progression*, as the term is used in Harmony, is the process of moving from one chord to the next one. The customary number of voices to be involved in the mechanics of a progression is four: soprano, alto, tenor, and bass. This is traditional, but fewer or more than four voices are not uncommon. Thus, the present text is confined exclusively to the technique of four-part harmony.

2. Progressions of triads fall into three general categories:

    (1) those having one common note,

    CEG   GBD

    (2) those having two common notes,

    CEG   EGB

    (3) and those that are without any common notes.

    CEG   DFA

3. These three general categories of progressions subdivide into six specific types that embrace every triadic relationship within the entire harmonic system:

(1) those having one common note,

(a) with roots ascending by 4th (descending by 5th)

I - IV
II - V
III - VI
IV - VII
V - I
VI - II
VII - III

(b) with roots descending by 4th (ascending by 5th)

I - V
II - VI
III - VII
IV - I
V - II
VI - III
VII - IV

(2) those having two common notes,

(a) with roots ascending by 3rd (descending by 6th)

I - III
II - IV
III - V
IV - VI
V - VII
VI - I
VII - II

(b) with roots descending by 3rd (ascending by 6th)

I - VI
II - VII
III - I
IV - II
V - III
VI - IV
VII - V

(3) and those that are without any common notes.

(a) with roots ascending by 2nd (descending by 7th)

I - II
II - III
III - IV
IV - V
V - VI
VI - VII
VII - I

(b) with roots descending by 2nd (ascending by 7th)

I - VII
II - I
III - II
IV - III
V - IV
VI - V
VII - VI

Thus, within the traditional system of major and minor keys there occur 42 specific triadic relationships which group themselves into six progression types which ultimately become crystallized into three general categories of progressions.

4. Basic principles for effecting the above progressions constitute the remainder of this chapter.

PROGRESSIONS HAVING ONE COMMON NOTE

5. A progression of this kind, both triads being in root position, can be effected through the following sequence of four steps:

Step 1: Construct the first of the two triads so that each chord member — Root, 3rd and 5th — comes in some upper voice.

Six arrangements of the three notes are available:

	1	2	3	4	5	6
Soprano:	5th	3rd	5th	3rd	Root	Root
Alto:	3rd	Root	Root	Root	5th	3rd
Tenor:	Root	5th	3rd	5th	3rd	5th

When the interval between tenor and soprano is less than an octave the chord is said to be in *close position*, but when this interval exceeds an octave it is then in *open position*. These two vertical spacing forms are illustrated by (a) and (b) above respectively,

3

Step 2: Keep the common note in the same voice and at the same pitch in the second chord as in the first chord, thereby producing a tied (or repeated) note against which the other three voices move.

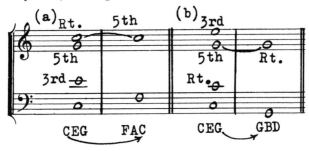

Step 3: Move the 3rd of the first chord stepwise and within the same voice to its nearest note in the second chord.

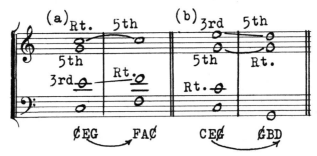

Step 4: Let the remaining note of the first chord move stepwise to its counterpart of the second chord, thereby completing the progression.

4

6. When the four steps shown in paragraph 5 above are correctly carried out, no leaps will occur in the three upper voices.

7. When several such progressions occur contiguously in an exercise or composition, *Step* 1 will take place automatically beginning with the second progression. That is to say, once the initial chord is structured and the first progression completed, only *Steps* 2, 3 *and* 4 need to be considered.

The above passage begins with the progression completed under (a) in paragraph 5 *Step* 4. It is left for the student to reconstruct *Steps* 2, 3 *and* 4 in the subsequent progressions.

PROGRESSIONS HAVING TWO COMMON NOTES

8. This kind of progression, with both triads in root position, requires but three steps:
Step 1: See *Step* 1 in paragraph 5.

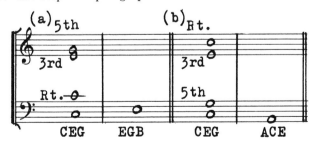

5

Step 2: Keep the two common notes in the same voices and at the same pitches in the second chord as in the first chord, thereby producing two tied (or repeated) notes against which the bass and one upper voice move.

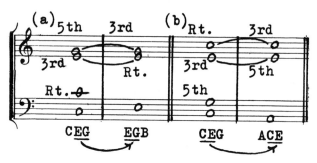

Step 3: Move the remaining note of the first chord stepwise to its counterpart in the second chord, thereby completing all voice-leadings in the progression.

9. The above sequence of progression steps will automatically produce three combinations of stepwise and tied (repeated note) voice-leadings in the soprano, alto and tenor parts:

	1	2	3
Soprano:	tie	tie	stepwise
Alto:	tie	stepwise	tie
Tenor:	stepwise	tie	tie

It is purely coincidental that both illustrations developed in paragraph 8 demonstrate the first arrangement.

6

10 When the three step process shown in paragraph 8 is correctly carried out, no leaps can occur in any of the three upper voices. (cf. paragraph 6.)

11. What is said about *Step* 1 in paragraph 7 is equally true of this progression type. (cf. paragraph 7.)

PROGRESSIONS HAVING NO COMMON NOTES

12. Progressions that contain no common notes are constructed by means of a two step process:

Step 1: Proceed as in *Step* 1 of paragraph 5. (cf. paragraphs 5 and 8.)

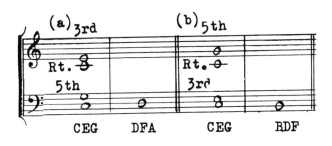

Step 2: The three upper voices will move — two stepwise and one by leap of a 3rd — from their positions in the first chord to their closest notes in the second chord in contrary motion to the direction of the bass.

7

This is our first instance of a leap in either the soprano, alto or tenor.
13. The three combinations of ties and stepwise motion as shown in paragraph 9 is now applicable to stepwise motion and leaps in the following way:

	1	2	3
Soprano:	stepwise	stepwise	leap
Alto:	stepwise	leap	·stepwise
Tenor:	leap	stepwise	stepwise

The progressions developed in paragraph 12 illustrate arrangements 2 and 3 at (a) and (b) respectively.

14. The six possible distributions of the three chord members within the three upper voices as listed in paragraph 5 are illustrated within the 12 chords of the six progressions developed in the foregoing illustrations thus:

	1st Chord	2nd Chord
paragraph 5 (a)	5	1
paragraph 5 (b)	2	3
paragraph 8 (a)	1	4
paragraph 8 (b)	6	2
paragraph 12 (a)	4	5
paragraph 12 (b)	3	6

15. A special condition must be placed upon the instructions given under *Step* 2 in paragraph 12. To move the three upper voices "in contrary motion to the direction of the bass" is valid only when the bass moves stepwise. When the bass leaps by 7th (cf. paragraph 3 (3)) this becomes impossible. When a 7th leap occurs in the bass it must be considered as a 2nd in the opposite direction to be properly harmonized; that is to say,

must be treated as follows.

16. When used in an exercise or practical composition the three general categories of progressions (cf. paragraph 3) are combined in any order desired by the composer as dictated by his artistic requirements. For instance, a harmonization of the following given bass

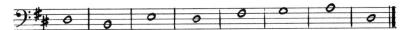

could be completed as shown in the solution below.

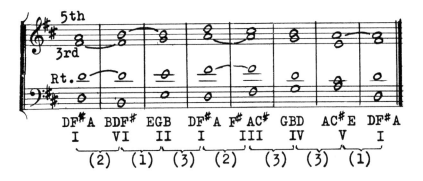

The figures in ( ) identify the type of progression according to the three categories as enumerated in paragraph 3.

17. The harmonization technique demonstrated in this chapter is the most elementary one, and is extremely restricted as regards chord structure and voice-leading. Thus, it would be rare to find an extended passage written within these limitations. Therefore, the following anonymous 16th century harmonization of a Chorale line is most unusual.

9

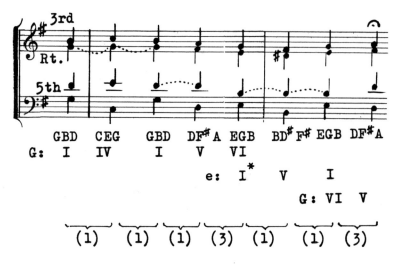

*The process of passing from one key to another by means of a common chord that occurs without chromatic alteration in both keys is known as Modulation and is treated in detail in Chapter XIV.

18. In the exercises for this and for succeeding chapters the vertical arrangement of the first chord is indicated either by no numeral or by a 3 or 5 above the initial note. When no numeral is given the root will go in the soprano (arrangements 5 or 6 in paragraph 5). A 3 tells that the 3rd goes in the soprano (arrangements 2 or 4), and 5 requires that the 5th be placed in the soprano (arrangements 1 or 3).

19. The exercises in minor keys will have a sharp or natural placed above the III or V notes. This accidental requires that the leading-tone will have to be raised as indicated when it serves as the 5th of the III triad and as 3rd in the V.

EXERCISES

Harmonize the following basses according to the instructions provided in this chapter. It would be in order to suggest that the arrangement of the initial chord be planned so that the tenor and bass will not cross during the course of the exercise.

11

CHAPTER II

BASIC PROGRESSION PRINCIPLES, CONTINUED

1. The present chapter is in effect an extension of Chapter I. Three special cases require separate consideration. These are as follows:
   (1) moving from one position to another within the same chord,
   (2) the II - V progression, and
   (3) the authentic cadence, i.e. the V - I progression, when the soprano melody descends stepwise to the final tonic.

MOVING FROM ONE POSITION TO ANOTHER WITHIN THE SAME CHORD

2. The principles set forth in Chapter I all concern the progression from a given chord to a different chord. However, any chord may be repeated freely with a different vertical arrangement of the three upper voices. No rules exist for such a repetition of the same chord. The following simple illustration comes from a 16th century Chorale harmonization.

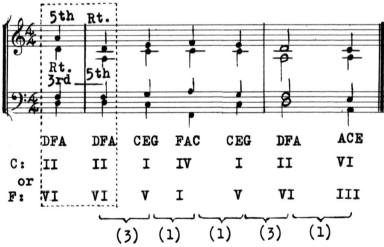

Since no B, natural or flat, occurs anywhere in the above harmonization the chords can be figured as being related to each other in either C or F major. This accounts for the double chord identification. It will be observed that the two opening chords are the same, the first being in vertical arrangement 3 and the second in vertical arrangement 5 as given in Chapter I, paragraph 5. From the second chord on all progressions are carried out in accordance with the instructions given in Chapter I. The progression types are identified as before.

3. There are no theoretical restrictions as to how many such chord repetitions may be used in a composition or at what points in a harmonization they may be placed. Usually, however, they are most apt to come at the beginning.

THE II - V PROGRESSION

4. The II - V progression has one common tone and is so listed under category (1)(a) in Chapter I, paragraph 3. For instance, in C major:

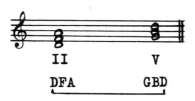

But it is generally not treated according to the instructions in paragraph 5 of Chapter I, but rather according to the no common tone (a) progression in paragraph 12. That is to say, move the notes in the three upper voices of II downward to their nearest notes in the V, as is shown below.

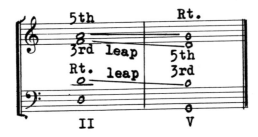

Herewith is set up a voice-leading combination not encountered in the progressions demonstrated in Chapter I; namely, two voices leaping by 3rd and one voice moving stepwise. Cf. Chapter I, paragraph 13.

5. Of course, when this progression is used to harmonize a melodic line that either repeats the 2nd degree of the scale or ascends stepwise from the 4th to the 5th degrees or from the 6th to the 7th degrees of the scale the instructions that are given above in paragraph 4 will obviously have to be ignored and the common tone kept intact in the same voice. These three specific melody harmonization requirements are illustrated in (a), (b) and (c) as given below.

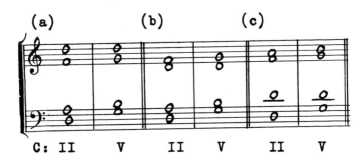

From the contrapuntal viewpoint the only objectionable progression above is (c) wherein the soprano and alto form the specific diagonal augmented 4th known as the *tritone*.

14

THE AUTHENTIC CADENCE WHEN THE SOPRANO
DESCENDS STEPWISE TO THE FINAL TONIC

6. When the soprano descends stepwise to the final tonic thus,

it becomes impossible to keep the common note in the V - I progression and proceed according to the instructions in paragraph 5 of Chapter I. Instead, apply what is shown in paragraph 4 above concerning the II - V progression. The same voice-leading combination will come about automatically.

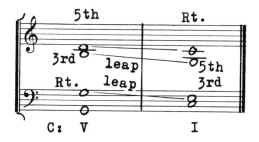

[1] See in FUNDAMENTAL COUNTERPOINT by Hugo Norden, paragraph 10 on page 12.

15

7. It will be observed that both of these progressions, II - V and V - I, are listed under (1) (a) in paragraph 3 of Chapter I.

8. Still another treatment of this cadential progression is possible by allowing the root and 5th of the V to move to the 3rd and root of the I as shown in paragraph 6, but letting the 3rd of the V ascend stepwise to the root of the I. This produces an incomplete I, having three roots and no 5th.

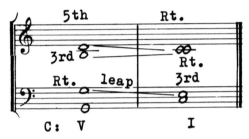

Here is yet another voice-leading combination: two voices moving stepwise in contrary motion while one leaps by 3rd.

9. How the three special cases that are the subject of this chapter can function within a harmonization is shown in the following passage. These are contained within the dotted lines for ready identification and for detailed examination. The remaining six progressions operate according to the basic principles spelled out in Chapter I. From the second chord on, this illustration is entirely in the open harmony format.

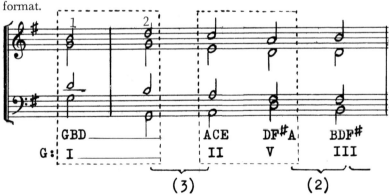

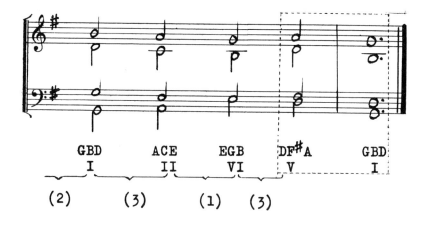

GBD   ACE   EGB   DF#A   GBD

I   II   VI   V   I

(2)   (3)   (1)   (3)

[1] Chapter I, paragraph 5, vertical arrangement 4.
[2] Chapter I, paragraph 5, vertical arrangement 3.

EXERCISES

Harmonize the following basses, noting especially the repeated chords, the II - V progressions, and the cadential V - I progressions, all of which are marked off by dotted lines. The cadential progressions may be treated either according to the instructions given in paragraph 5 of Chapter I or, optionally, in the two ways shown in paragraphs 6 - 8 above.

1.

2.

18

CHAPTER III

MELODY HARMONIZATION

1. All of the exercises in the first two chapters require that a harmonization be constructed above a given bass line. However, a composer will frequently harmonize a melody, and to this end he must provide a suitable harmony beneath it. With the resources made available in Chapters I and II, harmonization is possible only for melodies designed within the voice-leadings of the progressions. These, according to Chapter I, paragraph 3 and Chapter II, can be tabulated as follows:

Repeated note (9 *harmonization possibilities*):

    Root of a repeated chord

    3rd of a repeated chord

    5th of a repeated chord

    Root of 1st chord to 5th of 2nd chord in progression type (1) (a)

    5th of 1st chord to Root of 2nd chord in progression type (1) (b)

    3rd of 1st chord to Root of 2nd chord in progression type (2) (a)

    5th of 1st chord to 3rd of 2nd chord in progression type (2) (a)

    Root of 1st chord to 3rd of 2nd chord in progression type (2) (b)

    3rd of 1st chord to 5th of 2nd chord in progression type (2) (b)

2nd ascending (5 *harmonization possibilities*):

    3rd of 1st chord to Root of 2nd chord in progression type (1) (a)

    5th of 1st chord to 3rd of 2nd chord in progression type (1) (a)

    5th of 1st chord to Root of 2nd chord in progression type (2) (b)

    Root of 1st chord to 3rd of 2nd chord in progression type (3) (b)

    3rd of 1st chord to 5th of 2nd chord in progression type (3) (b)

2nd descending (5 *harmonization possibilities* + 2 *special cases*):
    Root of 1st chord to 3rd of 2nd chord in progression type (1) (b)
    3rd of 1st chord to 5th of 2nd chord in progression type (1) (b)
    Root of 1st chord to 5th of 2nd chord in progression type (2) (a)
    3rd of 1st chord to Root of 2nd chord in progression type (3) (a)
    5th of 1st chord to 3rd of 2nd chord in progression type (3) (a)

              *   *   *   *   *

    5th to Root in II - V progression
    5th to Root in cadential V - I progression
3rd ascending (3 *harmonization possibilities*):
    Root to 3rd of a repeated chord
    3rd to 5th of a repeated chord
    5th of 1st chord to Root of 2nd chord in progression type (3) (b)
3rd descending (3 *harmonization possibilities* + 2 *special cases*):
    3rd to Root of a repeated chord
    5th to 3rd of a repeated chord
    Root of 1st chord to 5th of 2nd chord in progression type (3) (a)

              *   *   *   *   *

    Root to 3rd in II - V progression
    3rd to 5th in II - V progression
    N.B. Both of these special cases will be Minor 3rds in either a
        major or minor key.
4th ascending:
    5th to Root of a repeated chord
4th descending:
    Root to 5th of a repeated chord
5th ascending:
    Same as 4th descending
5th descending:
    Same as 4th ascending
6th ascending:
    Same as first two possibilities for 3rd descending
6th descending:
    Same as first two possibilities for 3rd ascending
8ve ascending or descending:
    Same as first three possibilities for repeated note

Thus, from the progression and voice-leading resources established in Chapters I and II 43 harmony and soprano melody combinations become available.

2. It must be understood that what is tabulated above represents only the most limited and, in a sense, the most primitive melody-harmony resources. Not many extended passages can be found that operate strictly within these highly restrictive limitations. However, two Chorale lines from Hans Leo Hassler's "Kirkengesäng" (1608) show some of these possibilities in practical application.

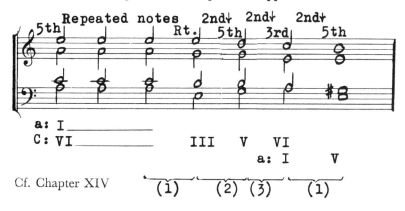

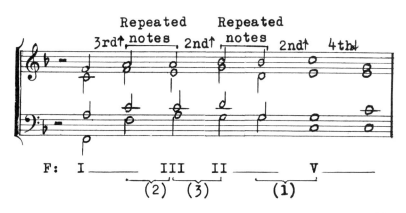

In the preceding quotation II - V is treated as a regular (1) (a) type progression, and *not* as the special case as given in Chapter II, paragraphs 4 - 5.

3. A typical problem would be to harmonize a melody such as the following line from a 16th century Chorale.

Before beginning the actual process of harmonization, identify all of the melodic intervals in the melody and determine the progression possibilities for each one from the table in paragraph 1.

4. The harmonization can be constructed in a series of three steps:
Step 1: Establish the cadential progression. For the present this will consist either of V - I (the *authentic cadence*) or IV - I (the *plagal cadence*). In the melody being treated herewith this will have to be IV - I because of the last two notes.

Obviously, the penultimate note of the melody, A, would not fit into the V triad (GBD), thereby leaving the IV triad (FAC) as the one to precede the terminal I cadentially.

22

Step 2: Treat the portion of the melody that offers the fewest progression possibilities. Consider herewith the third, fourth and fifth notes of the melody. See the progression possibilities for *3rd descending* and *3rd ascending* in paragraph 1 above. It will be seen that three treatments exist for these notes.

Version 1

Version 2

Version 3

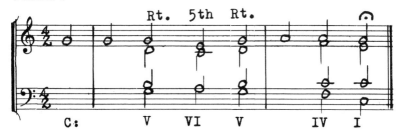

23

Step 3: Fill in suitable chords for the remaining notes, beginning with I.

Version 1

Version 2

Version 3

24

All three versions are equally correct academically. Which is the most successful musically is a matter of choice.

5. Melody harmonization is closely akin to puzzle solving in that it calls for the matching of suitable chord progressions to the notes of the given melody, both of which operate within a rigidly controlled framework of predetermined availabilities. In puzzle solving as well as in melody harmonization the number of choices is limited and could be calculated very quickly on a computer. But, in melody harmonization musical taste must go hand in hand with combinatorial ingenuity. It would be well to construct as many harmonizations as possible for each melody in order to be able to choose the best one. Here critical judgment enters.

EXERCISES

Harmonize the following melodies according to the resources made available in Chapters I and II.

1.

2.

3.

4.

5.

(I)   (I)

6.

(I)   (I)

CHAPTER IV

CHORDS OF THE SIXTH

1. Up to this point triads have been written only in root position; that is, with the root serving as bass. Herewith is being introduced the technique of employing triads with the 3rd as bass. A triad so arranged is known either as a *chord of the sixth* or a *triad in its first inversion*. The two terms are synonymous and interchangeable with no difference in meaning or usage.

2. The term *chord of the sixth* derives from the fact that when the 3rd becomes lowest note the root is a 6th above it.

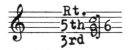

Actually, the complete figuration is $\frac{6}{3}$, but the 3 is used only when the 5th of the triad is chromaticized and therefore requires special identification.

27

Before proceeding to the technicalities involved in the use of chords of the sixth it might be helpful to examine a short passage containing them. The following is a Chorale line as harmonized by Hassler.

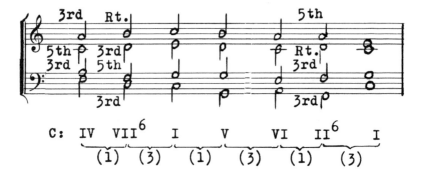

3. The above passage gives rise to four observations:
   (1) the first chord, IV, has the 3rd doubled,
   (2) the second and sixth chords are in the first inversion, with doubled 3rd,
   (3) the common note, F , in the first progression is kept sounding at the same pitch but not in the same voice,
   (4) the third and fourth progressions, embracing the third, fourth and fifth chords, follow implicitly the basic principles laid down in Chapter I.

It is now apparent that the use of chords of the sixth calls for greater freedom than has heretofore been available. However, this added freedom of chord formation and voice-leading within the progressions will be well controlled by the principles that follow.

DOUBLING

4. In the work of Chapters I - III there is never any question of doubling: the root is invariably doubled, coming in the bass and in one upper voice. But, the Hassler excerpt in paragraph 2 shows that

such a rigid doubling procedure is now impractical. However, the problem lies in attempting to arrive at a set of principles that are workable. This happens because composers so often have artistic objectives that conflict with the academic rules that the latter are often violated for greater creative freedom. Nevertheless, the following are generally valid:

in major triads (I, IV, V in major keys; V, VI in minor keys):
    root is best to double,
    5th is next best,
    3rd is least good (in the V triad the doubled 3rd should be avoided).

in minor triads (II, III, VI in major keys; I, IV in minor keys):
    any note may be doubled freely.

in diminished triads (VII in major keys; II, VII in minor keys):
    3rd is best to double,
    5th is next best,
    root is least good (in the VII triad the doubled root should be avoided).

in augmented triads (III in minor keys):
    3rd is best to double,
    root is next best,
    5th is least good and should be avoided.

In each case where avoidance is suggested this concerns the chord member that is the leading-tone.

5. It would be unrealistic to say that the doubling suggestion in paragraph 4 must be regarded as hard and fast "rules". Although many textbooks tend to give such an impression, the facts of the matter are that no competent and artistically creative composer would ever constrain himself by these academically traditional doubling limitations. Nevertheless, these doubling suggestions *do* reflect the practice of successful composers generally, and to this extent *do* merit serious consideration. A sampling of Chorale harmonizations by celebrated composers will give some idea as to how strictly the doubling suggestions in paragraph 4 are followed by men of great skill and unquestionable musical taste.

Bach

g: I ____ V⁶ I V VI II⁶ V ____

The doubled 3rd in the VI after V is a special case. Were these chords treated as a regular (3)(a) type progression (cf. Chapter I, paragraph 3), the 3rd of the V (i.e., the raised leading-tone) would descend to the root of the VI by an augmented 2nd, thereby creating a contrapuntally inadmissable voice-leading.

Hassler

F: I _____ V VI V⁶ VI⁶ II V

In the fifth chord, V⁶, the 3rd (i.e., the leading-tone) is doubled, thereby providing an interesting exception to what is said about doubling the 3rd of major triads — especially that of the V — in paragraph 4. By means of this doubling a two-fold imitation scheme becomes operative as indicated by the two kinds of dotted lines. Compare the closing progression of this quotation, II - V, with an identical case in the second illustration in paragraph 2 of Chapter III.

Schop

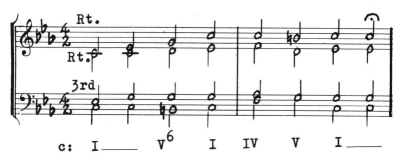

After the initial I without a 5th, this line proceeds without irregularities.

Scheidt

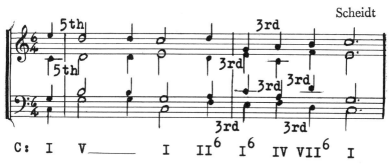

6. While no really meaningful statistics can be drawn from so small a sampling, these four Chorale lines by as many highly skilled composers do provide a basis for formulating an outlook. The following figures may be of interest:

(1) Out of a total of 34 chords 26 are in root position while 8 are in the first inversion.

(2) 23 have the root doubled, 7 the 3rd, and 4 the 5th.

(3) Of the 7 with the doubled 3rd only one, V, has the leading-tone doubled while two are diminished triads in the first inversion and have the best doubling, namely the 3rd.

(4) One of the 34 chords, a I triad, is incomplete, having three roots and a 3rd but no 5th.

31

Thus, while the doubling rules as given in paragraph 4 are put aside whenever a composer finds it necessary to do so, in the overall picture they are adhered to rather consistently. In other words, the student should heed these doubling rules conscientiously unless in some special situation he very honestly feels that he has a strong and valid reason for doing otherwise. Then he should feel free to do as his artistic sense dictates.

PARALLEL FIFTHS, OCTAVES AND UNISONS

7. Parallel 5ths, 8ves and unisons are not permitted in any of the six two-voice combinations that constitute a four-part harmony. This prohibition, never violated in academic harmony, is in an entirely dfferent class from the somewhat more elastic doubling rules.

8. In order to be incorrect the parallel intervals must appear in the same two-voice combination in two contiguous chords. In the following passage parallel 8ves come in the bass-soprano combination in addition to the parallel 5ths in bass-alto.

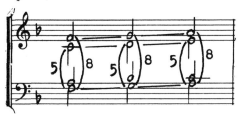

However, the faulty parallels can be eliminated by letting the bass and tenor cross at the second chord thus.

32

Now, although the notes are the same as in the preceding incorrect illustration, no parallel 5ths or 8ves are present in two contiguous chords in any of the six two-voice combinations:

bass - tenor
bass - alto
bass - soprano
tenor - alto
tenor - soprano
alto - soprano

From the above two illustrations is seen the operation of the TWO-VOICE PRINCIPLE:

In any multi-voiced structure, when all of the constituent two-voice combinations are correct, it follows that the structure as a whole is likewise correct.

9. The number of ways in which parallel 5ths, 8ves and unisons can occur is limited by a set of numerical facts. First, every pair of triads embodies nine voice-leadings:

(1) Root of 1st triad to Root of 2nd triad
(2) Root of 1st triad to 3rd of 2nd triad
(3) Root of 1st triad to 5th of 2nd triad
         *   *   *   *   *
(4) 3rd of 1st triad to Root of 2nd triad
(5) 3rd of 1st triad to 3rd of 2nd triad
(6) 3rd of 1st triad to 5th of 2nd triad
         *   *   *   *   *
(7) 5th of 1st triad to Root of 2nd triad
(8) 5th of 1st triad to 3rd of 2nd triad
(9) 5th of 1st triad to 5th of 2nd triad

It follows that in order to construct a correct four-part harmony, four different voice-leadings must be selected to operate at once. (The same voice-leading in two voices would result in parallel 8ves or unisons.) There are actually 126 4-out-of-9 combinations, but not all would make correct harmony.

10. Since there are 9 voice-leadings and 6 two-voice combinations in which any one of the 9 voice-leadings could be duplicated, it follows

that 54 (9 x 6) situations exist in which incorrect parallel 8ves or unisons might occur. And, since parallel 5ths happen only when voice-leading (1) is placed below (9) (as listed in paragraph 9), the 6 two-voice combinations can contain this error. Thus, one is 9 times as apt to make the error of parallel 8ves· or unisons as to write parallel 5ths.

11. Likewise to be avoided are consecutive 5ths and 8ves or unisons by contrary motion. While these effects are not too uncommon in textures for five and more voices, they are extremely rare in a four-part harmony. Nevertheless, below are given an example of each from the Chorale harmonizations of Hassler.

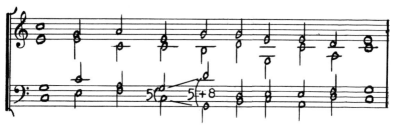

Such instances are highly unusual and, despite the composer's great fame, should not be emulated except for the most pressing artistic reasons.

12. In academic harmony the instruction is generally given to avoid so-called *hidden* 5ths, 8ves or unisons. This means simply to avoid

34

approaching a 5th, 8ve or unison by two voices moving in the same direction, especially if the two voices should leap. Such an approach to a perfect interval is especially bad if in the two outside voices. This whole matter can be completely ignored under two specific conditions:

(1) when one of the two voices involved moves stepwise, and
(2) when such a hidden 5th or 8ve occurs within different positions of the same chord, such as in the following:

Bach

What is said heretofore concerning DOUBLING and PARALLEL 5th, 8ves AND UNISONS provides ample background for proceeding with the successful employment of chords of the sixth.

13. A progression *to* a chord of the sixth *from* a triad in root position, of steps:

Step 1: Determine the notes of the two chords.

CEG   GBD

CEG   DFA

Step 2: Arrange the first chord. (cf. Chapter I, paragraph 5, *Step* 1)

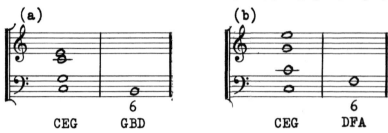

If the progression occurs at some point after the first chord, this step
or vice versa, can be worked out by means of the following series
will have taken place automatically. (cf. Chapter I, paragraph 7.)
Step 3: If a common note exists, keep it in the same voice; if not,
then move one voice stepwise.

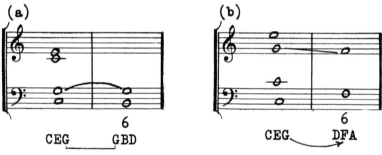

Step 4: Move one of the remaining voices stepwise.

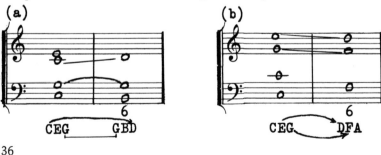

Step 5: Move the remaining voice either stepwise or by leap as desired.

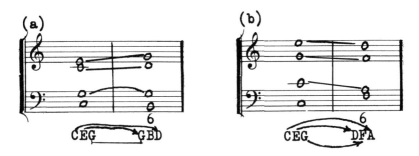

14. Other solutions for the above could be:

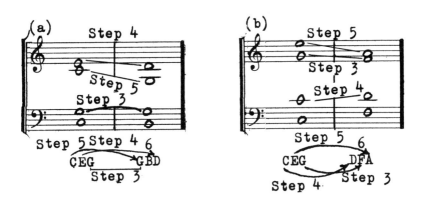

Considerable variety is possible in working out progressions, and some experimentation in this direction can prove highly rewarding. It may even make for a simple and entertaining computer problem.

15. Another doubling arrangement in the first chord could bring about other voice-leading combinations and thereby give the progression a different shape.

This, too, calls for further serious experimentation within the numerous varied doubling availabilities. (cf. paragraph 4.)

16. Should it be desired not to keep the common note in the same voice in progressions where either one or two such notes are available, it is certainly not obligatory to do so. In this case, the principles concerning doubling and parallel and hidden 5ths, 8ves and unisons should be most carefully observed. No violations in these matters are acceptable. However, it is expedient, whenever possible, in the absence of a common note to move at least one voice stepwise. The following would provide still another texturally suitable treatment of progression (a) above.

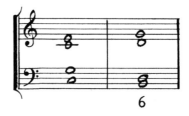

The available common note is not kept intact in the same voice, but the alto moves stepwise; and the 8ve between tenor and alto in the second chord is carefully approached by contrary motion.

17. When one chord of the sixth progresses to another triad also in the first inversion, the same order of steps is essentially operative. Care must be taken in the matter of doubling, especially when two major triads or a major and a diminished triad come contiguously. The following two Chorale quotations show how several chords of the sixth may be used in succession correctly and with good artistic effect.

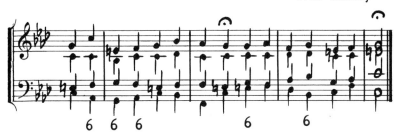

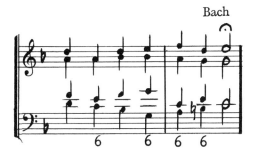

In studying the two illustrations given above it must be borne in mind that these harmonies were subjoined to a given melody so that the composers were not entirely free in their choice of voice-leadings and doublings. With this background try to reconstruct the steps through which each progression was constructed.

EXERCISES
Harmonize the following basses.

39

CHAPTER V

MELODY HARMONIZATION WITH CHORDS OF THE SIXTH

1. In Chapter III it was undertaken to harmonize melodies with the most meager of resources: triads in root position. With chords of the sixth available the possibilities for interesting harmonization are vastly increased in two respects:

(1) twice as many chord formations can now be used, and

(2) there is far greater freedom in voice-leading and doubling.

2. The process of harmonizing a melody should still begin with *Step* 1 of paragraph 4 in Chapter III. After that, the next important consideration should be the melodic flow of the bass line. In many of the 17th century Chorale books only the soprano melody and bass were given and it was left to the musicians to supply the tenor and alto parts.

3. At this point the first step might well be to list beneath a melody all chords available for each note thus:

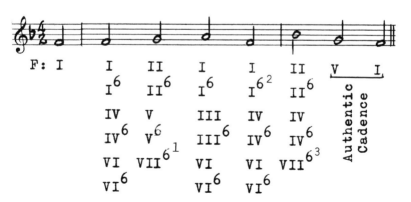

F: I   I   II   I   I   II   V   I

$$
\begin{array}{cccccc}
\text{I} & \text{II} & \text{I} & \text{I} & \text{II} & \text{V} \quad \text{I} \\
\text{I}^6 & \text{II}^6 & \text{I}^6 & \text{I}^{6\,2} & \text{II}^6 & \\
\text{IV} & \text{V} & \text{III} & \text{IV} & \text{IV} & \\
\text{IV}^6 & \text{V}^6 & \text{III}^6 & \text{IV}^6 & \text{IV}^6 & \\
\text{VI} & \text{VII}^{6\,1} & \text{VI} & \text{VI} & \text{VII}^{6\,3} & \\
\text{VI}^6 & & \text{VI}^6 & \text{VI}^6 & &
\end{array}
$$

Authentic Cadence

41

[1] Diminished triads are generally not used in root position unless the composer has a specific reason for doing so.

[2] Would tend to create an unsatisfactory doubling.

[3] A stronger cadential effect is generally achieved by not preceding the penultimate V by another V or VII harmony.

4. From this list of available chords the composer will select those that in his estimation produce the most effective harmonization. Two possible unpretentious harmonizations with chords selected from the above availabilities follow.

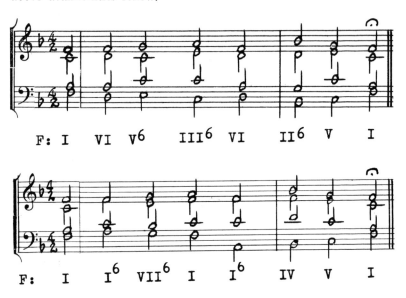

F: I   VI   V6   III6   VI   II6   V   I

F: I   I6   VII6   I   I6   IV   V   I

Which is the more successful is, of course, a matter of choice. Both are equally "correct".

EXERCISES

The following melodies to be harmonized are selected from the classical Chorale literature. All have been successfully harmonized by numerous composers.

42

43

Chapter VI

THE SIX-FOUR CHORD

1. Before proceeding with the work of the present chapter, look ahead to the chapter on NON-HARMONIC NOTES and read about passing-notes, auxiliary-notes, dual passing-notes, suspensions and the appoggiatura since what follows herewith relates to that material.

2. The so-called *six-four chord* is a triad in its second inversion; that is, with the 5th in the bass. It derives its name from the intervals that comprise its formation.

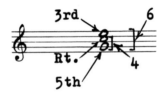

In the strictest harmonic sense this is not actually a chord. It comes closer to being a sort of harmonic illusion resulting from tightly controlled combinations of specific discords. This is due to the fact that in Counterpoint a 4th above the bass is always a discord.* There are basically three kinds of six-fours.

*See in FUNDAMENTAL COUNTERPOINT by Hugo Norden, footnote 1) on page 25.

THE PEDAL-POINT SIX-FOUR

3. This kind of six-four chord is formed by two upward auxiliary-notes within a root position triad. These two auxiliary-notes invariably move *from* and *to* the 3rd and 5th of the triad respectively.

When embellished in this way the three upper voices can still be placed in any of the six vertical arrangements that are listed in paragraph 5 of Chapter I. Translated into simple chords the above passage would appear thus:

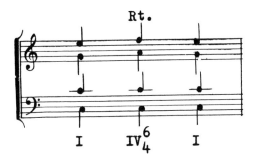

The auxiliary-note to the 3rd of the original triad becomes the root of the six-four chord.

4. Such a six-four chord is a relatively weak effect and is found only very rarely in serious music. The following is an unusual instance in a Chorale by Scheidt.

$$d\colon \quad I \rule{1cm}{0.4pt} IV^6_4 \ I \ IV$$

THE PASSING SIX-FOUR

5. The passing six-four is constructed by means of two passing-notes and one auxiliary-note between a triad in root position and the same chord in its first inversion arranged thus,

or in retrograde.

The discords are inserted in the following way.

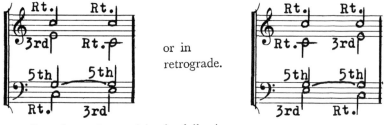

46

6. As chords the above passages appear as follows:

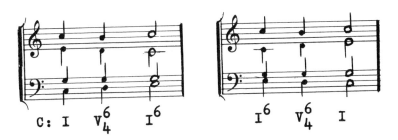

The 5th of the original triad becomes the root of the six-four.

7. Like the pedal-point six-four, the passing six-four is not a particularly strong harmonic device and good examples are difficult to find. The following pair of simple quotations from well known hymns are fairly typical.

THE CADENTIAL TONIC SIX-FOUR

8. The pedal-point and passing six-four effects have two structural characteristics that are not shared by the cadential I_4^6 :

    (1) they are generally built *within* I harmony, and

    (2) they are, theoretically, unaccented rhythmically.

The cadential I_4^6 is built around V harmony and is invariably accented. It comes into being as a double suspension or appoggiatura above the 3rd and 5th of the V triad.

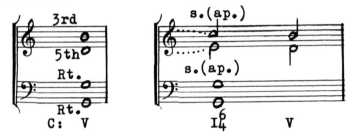

9. This is the commonest of cadential clichés and abounds in the music of all sorts of composers. The following are a few Chorale excerpts picked at random.

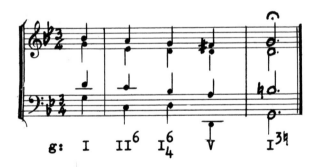

[1] The chromatically raised 3rd in a terminal I triad in a minor key is sometimes known as the *Tierce de Picardie.*

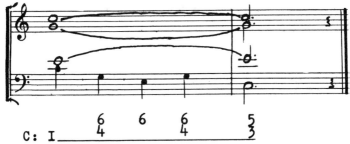

Although simple, the last illustration is interesting in one respect. If the I_4^6 is considered as a double appoggiatura to the V triad (cf. paragraph 8) and not as a chord, then there is actually only one harmony per measure.

THE ARPEGGIO SIX-FOUR

10. The so-called "arpeggio" six-four is not a chord at all, and its traditional inclusion in textbooks may well be thought of as a mistake. It comes about inadvertently when the notes of a triad function melodically in the bass. The same kind of passage will undoubtedly yield a chord of the sixth as well.

Two examples from familiar patriotic songs show such six-four formations in use in practical compositions.

America

F: I   6   6   5
         4   3

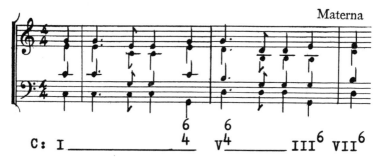

Materna

C: I   6   6   III⁶   VII⁶
       4   V4

In the discussions to come no mention is made of the arpeggio six-four
since this is not a valid chord in the contrapuntal sense and therefore
requires no further consideration.

11. It must not be assumed that all usage of six-four chords is as
simple and unadorned as the illustrations given in this chapter. A
resourceful composer will seek ways to embellish and, when he so
desires, to disguise conventional chords by non-harmonic effects,
rhythmic displacements, etc. But, what *is* shown adequately here is
the principle through which six-four chords come into being and by
which they are properly manipulated. This general principle can be
summarized thus:

> If a six-four chord can be analyzed also as a combination of
> correctly treated discords operating within a larger harmonic
> framework, then it can safely be considered as a correctly treated
> six-four both in structure and operation.

50

12. To harmonize a bass containing six-four chords, such as the following,

proceed according to the following order of steps:
Step 1: Identify and write in the six-four patterns. (It is generally expedient to place them in approximately the same register.)

Step 2: Fill in the remaining chords.

EXERCISES

Following the suggestions given in paragraph 12, harmonize the basses given below.

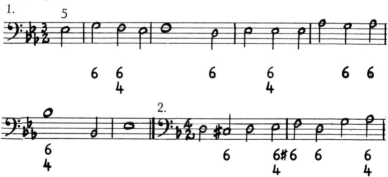

52

3.

4.

Chapter VII

MELODY HARMONIZATION WITH SIX-FOUR CHORDS

1. To harmonize a melody with six-four chords it is necessary to identify melodic figures against which a six-four pattern will fit. There are nine figures consisting of three notes and three of two notes, and each has its own specific harmonization possibilities. These figures and their respective chords must all be clearly kept in mind to avoid confusion when undertaking a melody harmonization. A fairly complete listing follows. However, while all of the following are possible, only those involving the primary triads (I, IV, V) are to be found in traditional usage.

(1) *Repeated notes*

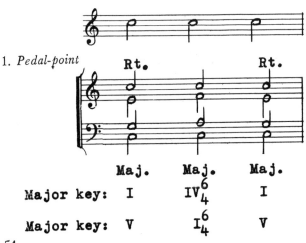

	Maj.	Maj.	Maj.
Major key:	I	IV$_4^6$	I
Major key:	V	I$_4^6$	V

54

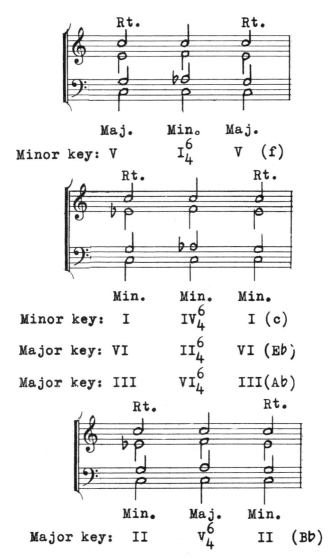

Minor key: V   I$^6_4$ V   (f)
               Maj.   Min.   Maj.

Minor key: I   IV$^6_4$ I   (c)
               Min.   Min.   Min.

Major key: VI   II$^6_4$ VI (E♭)

Major key: III   VI$^6_4$ III (A♭)

Major key: II   V$^6_4$ II (B♭)
               Min.   Maj.   Min.

Very unlikely and musically dubious.

2. *Passing*

Maj.Maj.Maj.   Maj.Maj.Maj.

Major key: I V_4^6 I^6 I^6 V_4^6 I (F)

Major key: IV I_4^6 IV^6 IV^6 I_4^6 IV (C)

Min.Maj.Min.   Min.Maj.Min.

Minor key: I V_4^6 I^6 I^6 V_4^6 I (f)

Min. Min. Min.   Min. Min. Min.

Minor key: IV I_4^6 IV^6 IV^6 I_4^6 IV (c)

Major key: II VI_4^6 II^6 II^6 VI_4^6 II (Eb)

Major key: VI III_4^6 VI^6 VI^6 III_4^6 VI (Ab)

Major key: V   II$_4^6$ V^6 V^6 II$_4^6$ V   (B♭)

Highly unlikely and questionable musically.

(2) *Descending arc in minor 2nds*

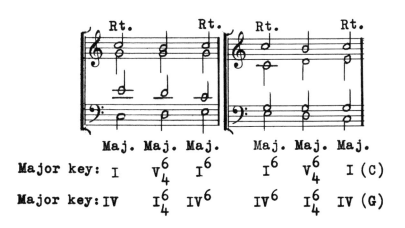

Major key: I   V$_4^6$ I^6 I^6 V$_4^6$ I (C)

Major key: IV   I$_4^6$ IV^6 IV^6 I$_4^6$ IV (G)

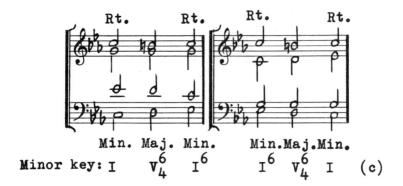

Min. Maj. Min.   Min. Maj. Min.

Minor key: I   V$_4^6$ I^6 I^6 V$_4^6$ I   (c)

(3). *Descending arc in major 2nds*

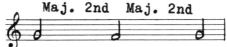

Maj. 2nd   Maj. 2nd

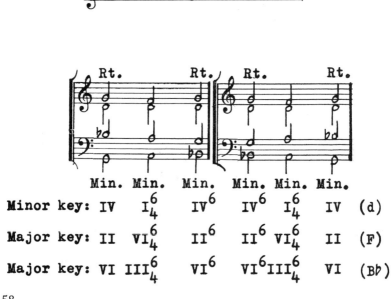

Min. Min. Min.   Min. Min. Min.

Minor key: IV   I$_4^6$ IV^6 IV^6 I$_4^6$ IV   (d)

Major key: II   VI$_4^6$ II^6 II^6 VI$_4^6$ II   (F)

Major key: VI   III$_4^6$ VI^6 VI^{6}III$_4^6$ VI   (B♭)

58

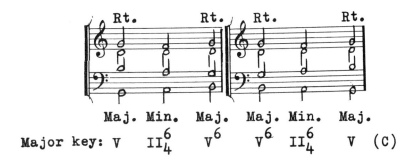

Major key: V II_4^6 V^6 V^6 II_4^6 V   (C)

Highly unlikely.

    (4) *Ascending arc in minor 2nds*

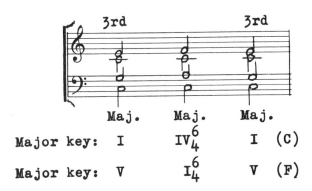

Major key: I IV_4^6 I   (C)

Major key: V I_4^6 V   (F)

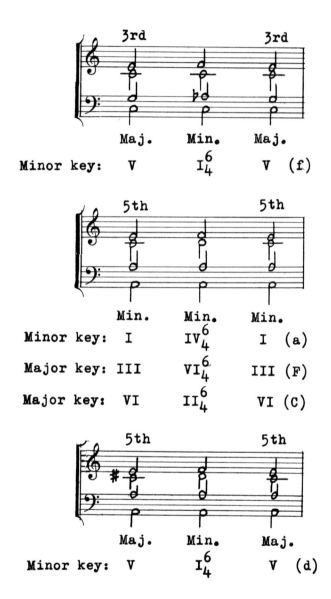

Minor key: V   I$_4^6$ V (f)

Min.   Min.   Min.
Minor key: I   IV$_4^6$ I (a)
Major key: III   VI$_4^6$ III (F)
Major key: VI   II$_4^6$ VI (C)

Maj.   Min.   Maj.
Minor key: V   I$_4^6$ V (d)

(5) *Ascending arc in major 2nds*

Minor key:	I	IV$_4^6$ (Min.)	I (e)
Major key:	III	VI$_4^6$ (Min.)	III (C)
Major key:	VI	II$_4^6$ (Min.)	VI (G)

Major key:	II	V$_4^6$ (Maj.)	II (D)

Highly unlikely.

Major key: I   IV⁶₄   I   (C)

Major key: V   I⁶₄   V   (F)

Major key: II   V⁶₄   II   (B♭)

Most unlikely and contrapuntally inept.

(6) *Descending line by major 2nds*

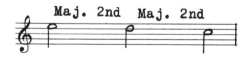

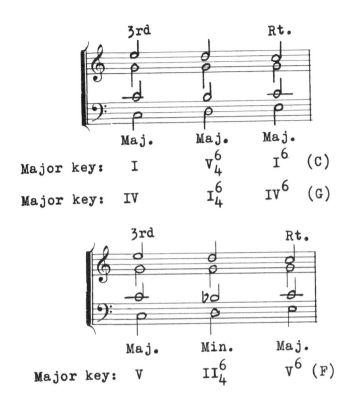

		Maj.	Maj.	Maj.	
Major key:	I		V_4^6	I^6	(C)
Major key:	IV		I_4^6	IV^6	(G)

		Maj.	Min.	Maj.	
Major key:	V		II_4^6	V^6	(F)

Unlikely and inept.

(7) *Ascending line by major 2nds*

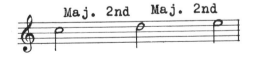

Same harmonic patterns as for descending line by major 2nds but taken in retrograde.

(8) *Descending line by minor - major 2nds*

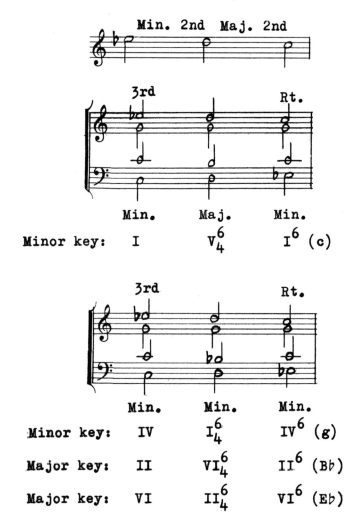

| Minor key: | I | V$^6_4$ | I^6 (c) |

Minor key:	IV	I$^6_4$	IV^6 (g)
Major key:	II	VI$^6_4$	II^6 (B♭)
Major key:	VI	II$^6_4$	VI^6 (E♭)

(9) *Ascending line by major - minor 2nds*

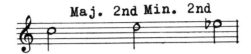

Same harmonic patterns as for descending line by minor - major 2nds but taken in retrograde.

(10) *Two-note figures in cadential I$^6_4$ - V progression*

1. *Repeated note*

2. *Descending by minor 2nd*

Major key: I_4^6 V   (c)

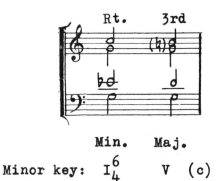

Minor key: I_4^6 V   (c)

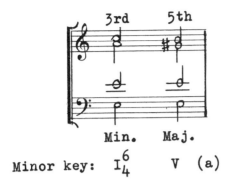

Minor key: I$_4^6$ V (a)

3. *Descending by major 2nd*

Major key: I$_4^6$ V (c)

2. From the above list it will be seen that within the academic framework of six-four usage there are 12 melodic figures that fit into 62 specific harmonic patterns. But, as already mentioned in paragraph 1, only those operating within the primary triads are to be found in common traditional usage.

3. The process for harmonizing a melody with six-four chords can be carried out by means of the following series of steps:
Step 1: Identify all six-four opportunities in the melodic line.

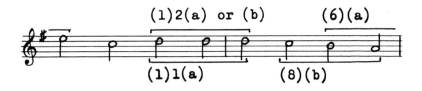

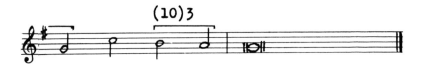

Step 2: Select those figures that seem to be artistically valid and put in place.

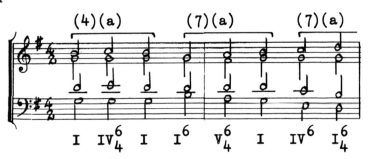

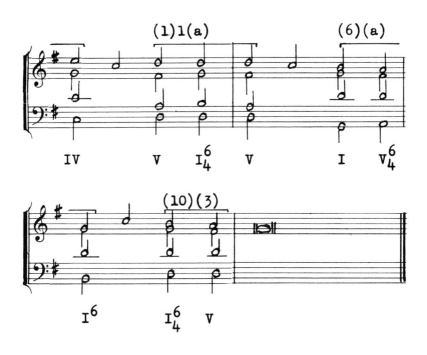

Step 3. Fill in the remaining chords.

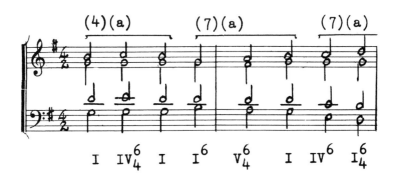

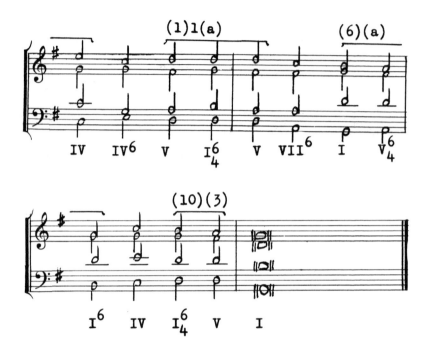

It goes without saying that this is a synthetic melody and for purposes of illustration is vastly overloaded with six-four clichés. It may be discovered that six-four chords are most effective when used sparingly.
4. It must not be assumed that composers are always as rigid in observing the contrapuntal character of six-four movement as what is shown in this chapter might lead one to believe. An entertaining research project might be to read through Bach's 371 Chorales and see how many irregular six-four treatments one can find.

EXERCISES

Harmonize the following melodies, using six-four chords wherever they fit in gracefully and are artistically successful.

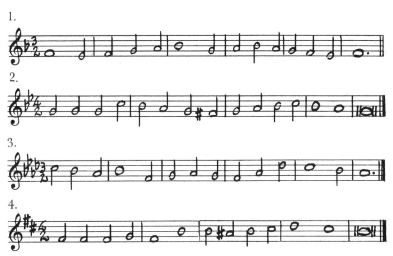

Invent original melodies containing six-four figures and harmonize same.

CHAPTER VIII

NON-HARMONIC NOTES

1. A *non-harmonic note* is a note that is alien to a chord and is sounded against the chord under tightly controlled conditions of movement into and away from the resulting dissonance.

2. Non-harmonic notes have two purposes to serve:

   (1) to strengthen a progression or activate a chord repetition by effecting a dissonating stepwise movement from one chord to another, and

   (2) to embellish dissonantly a chord note.

These two categories of non-harmonic notes and their several uses will be treated separately.

CONNECTING OR DIRECTIONAL DISSONANCES

3. There are seven directional dissonances, each with a specific connecting function:

   (1) *Auxiliary-note*: connects two concords at the same pitch.

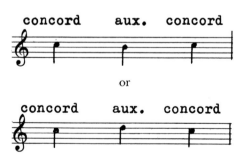

(2) *Ascending passing-note*: connects two concords a 3rd apart upwards.

(3) *Descending passing-note*: connects two concords a 3rd apart downwards.

(4) *Ascending dual passing-notes*: connects two concords a 4th apart upwards.

(5) *Descending dual passing-notes*: connects two concords a 4th apart downwards.

(6) *Suspension*: strengthens a progression by delaying a voice descending by a 2nd.

(7) *Retardation*: strengthens a progression by delaying a voice ascending by a 2nd.

Usually the retardation is limited to voice-leadings that ascend by a minor 2nd, although this restriction is not obligatory.

4. An eighth directional discord is the *anticipation* which amounts to nothing more than a suspension or retardation in reverse; namely, the second note being struck briefly ahead of time.

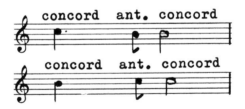

EMBELLISHING OR NON-DIRECTIONAL DISCORDS

5. There are essentially two types of embellishing discords. These are the *appoggiatura*, which embellishes the beginning of a note, and the *échappée*, which embellishes the end of a note. Each of these two

74

discords must, however, be subdivided into those that ascend and those that descend to or from the chord member.

(1) *Descending appoggiatura*: an accented discord a major or minor 2nd above a note of a chord.

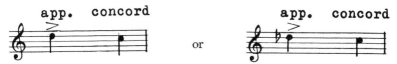

or

(2) *Ascending appoggiatura*: an accented discord which comes a minor 2nd below a note of a chord.

(3) *Échappée above a chord member*: an unaccented discord a major or minor 2nd above a note of a chord.

or

(4) *Échappée below a chord member*: an unaccented discord a major or minor 2nd below a note of a chord.

or

The échappée can best be thought of as an appoggiatura effect in reverse.

6. What follows in this chapter concerns only the connecting or directional dissonances. Consideration of the embellishing discords is being deferred until Chapter XV.

AUXILIARY-NOTES, PASSING-NOTES AND DUAL PASSING-NOTES WITHIN THE SAME TRIAD

7. Within any triad the following directional non-harmonic notes are available:

> 6 auxiliary-notes
> 4 passing-notes
> 2 dual passing-notes

These 12 dissonating effects operate within a triad as is shown below in the C major chord.

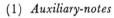

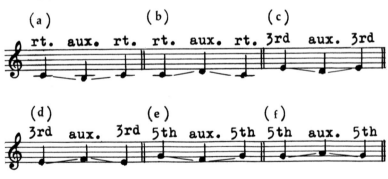

(2) *Passing-notes*

(3) *Dual passing-notes*

These may be used singly or they can be combined in various ways so long as they do not produce any parallel 5ths, 8ves or unisons. An assortment of varied illustrations from the Bach 371 Chorales follows.

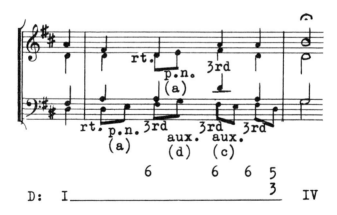

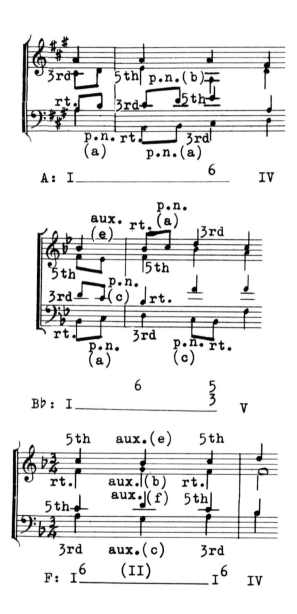

These quadruple auxiliary-notes form another harmony *within* the original triad. Compare the six-four effects in Chapters VI and VII. These can all be identified as specific auxiliary-notes and passing-notes.

NON-HARMONIC NOTES IN PROGRESSIONS

8. Every pair of triads embodies nine voice-leadings (cf. Chapter IV, paragraph 9.) There are six types of triadic relationships. (cf. Chapter I, paragraph 3.) From these two facts it follows that the triadic system offers 54 situations wherein directional discords can function. These are as follows:

(1) (*a*) *roots ascending by 4th (descending by 5th)*:
    Root - Root — dual passing-notes up*
    Root - 3rd — passing-note down
    Root - 5th — auxiliary-note

    3rd - Root — retardation
    3rd - 3rd — dual passing-notes up*
    3rd - 5th — passing-note down

    5th - Root — suspension
    5th - 3rd — retardation
    5th - 5th — dual passing-notes up

(1) (*b*) *roots descending by 4th (ascending by 5th)*:
    Root - Root — dual passing-notes down
    Root - 3rd — suspension
    Root - 5th — retardation

    3rd - Root — passing-note up
    3rd - 3rd — dual passing-notes down*
    3rd - 5th — suspension

    5th - Root — auxiliary-note
    5th - 3rd — passing-note up
    5th - 5th — dual passing-notes down*

*Dual passing-notes in effect only, the second note in the figure being a member of the first triad.

79

(2) (*a*) *roots ascending by 3rd (descending by 6th)* :

Root - Root — passing-note up
Root - 3rd — dual passing-notes down
Root - 5th — suspension

3rd - Root — auxiliary-note
3rd - 3rd — passing-note up
3rd - 5th — dual passing-notes down*

5th - Root — passing-note down
5th - 3rd — auxiliary-note
5th - 5th — passing-note up

(2) (*b*) *roots descending by 3rd (ascending by 6th)* :

Root - Root — passing-note down
Root - 3rd — auxiliary-note
Root - 5th — passing-note up

3rd - Root — dual passing-notes up*
3rd - 3rd — passing-note down
3rd - 5th — auxiliary-note

5th - Root — retardation
5th - 3rd — dual passing-notes up
5th - 5th — passing-note down

*Dual passing-notes in effect only, the second note in the figure being a member of the first triad.

(3) (*a*) *roots ascending by 2nd (descending by 7th)* :

Root - Root — retardation
Root - 3rd — dual passing-notes up*
Root - 5th — passing-note down

3rd - Root — suspension
3rd - 3rd — retardation
3rd - 5th — dual passing-notes up*

5th - Root — dual passing-notes down*
5th - 3rd — suspension
5th - 5th — retardation

80

(3) (b) *roots descending by 2nd (ascending by 7th)*:

Root - Root — suspension
Root - 3rd — retardation
Root - 5th — dual passing-notes up*

3rd - Root — dual passing-notes down*
3rd - 3rd — suspension
3rd - 5th — retardation

5th - Root — passing-note up
5th - 3rd — dual passing-notes down*
5th - 5th — suspension

*Dual passing-notes in effect only, the second note in the figure being a member of the first triad.

9. Three restrictions will insure the proper usage of directional non-harmonic notes:

(1) when a note common to the 5th of the second triad is kept in the same voice against a voice moving stepwise to the root, an auxiliary-note within the common note must not approach the 5th in parallel motion with the moving voice thereby producing parallel 5ths.

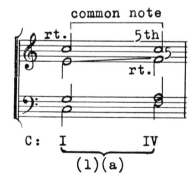

(1)(a)

Bad!

Good!

(2) when a progression contains a hidden 5th, 8ve or unison (cf. Chapter IV, paragraph 12), passing-notes must not be inserted into a leap, or leaps, so as to produce parallel 5ths, 8ves or unisons.

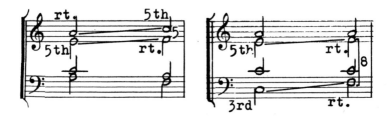

Both bad!

(3) a suspension must not resolve to a note that is doubled in any voice except in the bass. This precaution will avoid a 9 - 8 suspension between any pair of upper voices or a 7 - 8 effect anywhere.

Bad!

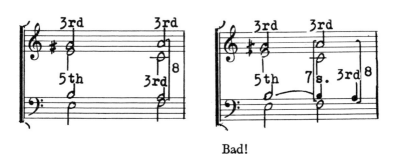

Bad!

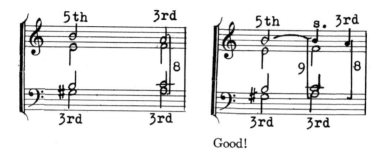

Good!

10. Possibilities for the artistic employment of non-harmonic notes, both within the same triad and in progressions, are virtually unlimited. While the non-harmonic notes available are only those listed in paragraph 8, their placement and design within a time span offers combinatorial opportunities to test the inventiveness of the most resourceful composer. The following assortment of Chorale quotations by several skilled composers are typical.

Scheidt

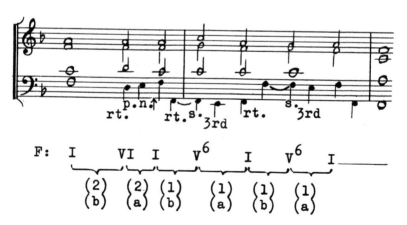

Alternative analysis of third chord:

85

With non-harmonic notes it becomes possible, as shown by the preceding double analysis of a Bach passage, to make an art of achieving ambiguity in the harmonic fabric and the dissonances. By this means the square-cut effect of straight chordal harmony is modified.

11. So much variety is available in the usage of non-harmonic notes that it would be impossible even to approach a comprehensive and meaningful demonstration within the space of a few pages. With the above illustrations serving as introduction, the student is urged to examine as much music as possible in order to become aware of composers' efforts and achievements in this direction. It should be noted that when non-harmonic notes are in operation, composers are likely to be considerably more free in the matter of doubling in order to achieve greater linear fluency. (cf. Chapter IV, paragraph 4.)

12. More sophisticated concepts of non-harmonic note usage are put forth in the chapters on Chords of the Seventh and of the Ninth.

THE PEDAL-POINT

13. The *pedal-point* derives its name from the pedals of the organ, whereby a highly idiomatic effect is to hold a pedal note and then play various harmonies, related or unrelated, above it. Actually, while most pedal-points probably do occur in the bass, there is no reason why such a sustained (or repeated) note cannot be placed in any voice provided it gives the desired musical effect. Only one "rule" exists for correct pedal-point usage; namely, that the beginning and end of the pedal-point should harmonize with the accompanying chords which may be placed above, around or below it. What takes place along the way is largely immaterial and completely free. The following simple examples from Scheidt will suffice.

V_____V I
pedal-point

pedal-point

14. It can be argued that neither of the above illustrations are true pedal-points in the academic sense in that no chords are played against the pedal note that do not include it as a chord member. From this point of view, the following — although contrived for illustration purposes — may be a more valid demonstration of the pedal-point principle.

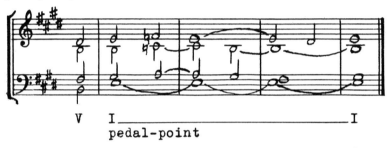

V   I_____I
pedal-point

15. Double pedal-points are also quite possible and may be placed in any of the six two-voice combinations listed in paragraph 8 of Chapter IV.

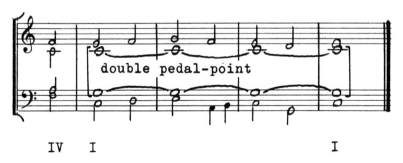

double pedal-point

IV   I   I

87

Of course, pedal-points — if too greatly overdone — can very easily become crude and ineffective.

EXERCISES

I. Identify all chords, non-harmonic notes, and progression types in the following Chorale lines.

II. Rework any exercises given in the foregoing chapters, using non-harmonic notes where possible.

CHAPTER IX

CHORDS OF THE SEVENTH

1. A *chord of the seventh* consists of four notes and is named from the interval between its root and highest note.

Unlike a triad, such a chord contains a dissonance between two of its members.

2. Such a chord can be seen structurally from three quite different viewpoints:

(1) as three vertically aligned 3rds,

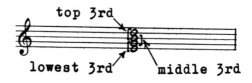

(2) as a triad with a superimposed 3rd, or

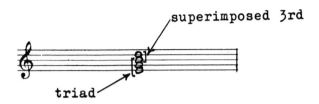

(3) as two triads in progression type (2). (cf. Chapter I, paragraph 3.)

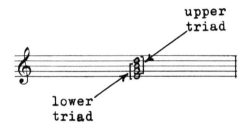

The four chord members are named root, 3rd, 5th, and 7th respectively.

3. Seven different kinds of chords of the seventh are intervalically possible. Their structures and functions are as follows:

(1)

Major Key: I⁷, IV⁷
Minor Key: VI⁷

(2)

Major and Minor Key: V⁷
Minor Key with raised 6th degree (Melodic Minor Scale): IV⁷

(3)

Major Key: II⁷, III⁷, VI⁷
Minor Key: IV⁷
Minor Key with raised 6th degree (Melodic Minor Scale): II⁷

(4)

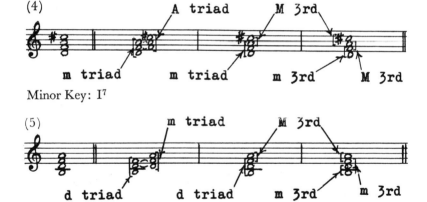

Minor Key: I⁷

(5)

Major Key: VII⁷
Minor Key: II⁷
Minor Key with raised 6th degree (Melodic Minor Scale): VI⁷

(6)

d triad   m 3rd

d triad   d triad   m 3rd   m 3rd

Minor Key: VII⁷

(7)

M triad   m 3rd

A triad   A triad   M 3rd   M 3rd

Minor Key: III⁷

A chord of the seventh in which are combined two major triads, two minor triads or two augmented triads is structurally impossible.

4. The distribution of these seven kinds of chords of the seventh within the major and minor keys can be seen from the following:

Major Key:

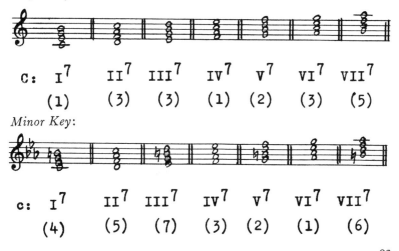

c:	I⁷	II⁷	III⁷	IV⁷	V⁷	VI⁷	VII⁷
	(1)	(3)	(3)	(1)	(2)	(3)	(5)

Minor Key:

c:	I⁷	II⁷	III⁷	IV⁷	V⁷	VI⁷	VII⁷
	(4)	(5)	(7)	(3)	(2)	(1)	(6)

93

When the raised 6th degree of the melodic minor scale is used harmonically, II⁷ becomes changed from type (5) to type (3), IV⁷ from type (3) to type (2), and VI⁷ from type (1) to type (5); which merely restates portions of paragraph 3.

5. Any chord of the seventh will be resolved correctly and musically when the following voice-leading principles are rigorously heeded:

    (1) the 7th should resolve either (a) by step downward or (b) by tie to a common note in the subsequent chord, whether the latter is a triad or another chord of the seventh,

    (2) when the interval between the root and 5th is a diminished 5th, as in types (5) and (6), the 5th should also be resolved either (a) by step downward or (b) by tie to a common note in the next chord,

    (3) any leading-tone should resolve by step upward whenever possible,

    (4) any other notes of a chord of the seventh may move freely into the next chord either by step, by tie or by leap, being in effect neutral notes with no fixed resolution tendencies requiring special consideration.

The above principles for resolving chords of the seventh do require some further comment.

6. The 7th can be resolved by step downward if the chord of the seventh progresses to

    (1) a triad or chord of the seventh a 2nd above (or 7th below), resolving to the 5th,

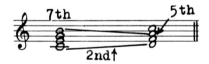

(2) a triad or chord of the seventh a 4th above (or 5th below), resolving to the 3rd,

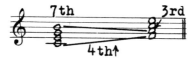

(3) a triad or chord of the seventh a 6th above (or 3rd below), resolving to the root,

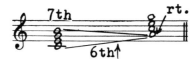

(4) a chord of the seventh a 2nd below (or 7th above), resolving to the 7th.

On the other hand, it will resolve by tie (or note repetition) when the chord of the seventh progresses to
(1) a triad or chord of the seventh a 3rd above (or 6th below), resolving to the 5th,

(2) a triad or chord of the seventh a 5th above (or 4th below), resolving to the 3rd,

(3) a triad or chord of the seventh a 7th above (or 2nd below), resolving to the root (cf. (4) above).

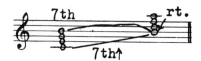

7. Item (3) in paragraph 5 creates a special problem in one specific instance, in the I⁷ in a minor key (cf. paragraph 3, type (4)). In this particular case the 7th of the chord is the raised leading-tone which cannot very well resolve downward because the interval of resolution would unavoidably be an augmented 2nd. Except for this unique situation, no exceptions to the resolution principles as given in paragraph 5 need be anticipated.

8. A few typical Bach passages employing chords of the seventh follow.

---

[1] 7th "prepared" by tie from (or by repeating) the same note in the preceding chord.

[2] V^6 can be viewed as triple passing-notes between I and VI^7.

[3] See paragraph 5 (2).

[4] See Chapter II, paragraph 6.

97

9. Although it is unnecessary at this point to institute a series of fixed steps in order to harmonize a given bass such as the following,

a systematic procedure such as is illustrated below might prove helpful in treating correctly the more complex textures occasioned by the chords of the seventh:

(1) determine whether it will be possible to prepare the 7th by tying (or repeating) a common note in the preceding chord,

(2) determine whether the 7th will have to be resolved by tie (or repeated note) or by descending stepwise into the next chord,

(3) identify the leading-tones in the chords of the seventh and determine whether they can be resolved successfully stepwise upward. (This is desirable but never obligatory except in certain minor key situations.)

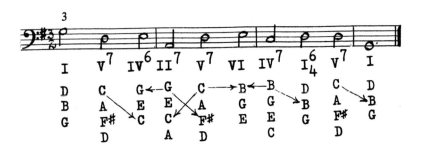

Being cognizant of the circumstances governing the progression into and the resolution of each chord of the seventh as shown in the above diagram, the harmonization can be completed as follows:

The fifth chord, V^7 in the second measure, requires two observations concerning liberties taken for better texture and smoother voice-leading:

(1) the 7th (C in tenor) is placed in a different voice and an 8ve lower than its common note in the preceding chord, and

(2) the leading-tone (F-sharp in alto) descends stepwise in order to achieve a richer sounding structure in the VI triad.

10. The V^7 - I progression is often treated in a special way in order to obtain a complete I triad; namely, to omit the 5th and double the root in the V^7 and then tie the root that comes in an upper voice to the 5th of the I. By this method the harmonization in paragraph 9 could end as follows:

EXERCISES

Harmonize the following basses.

CHAPTER X

INVERSIONS OF CHORDS OF THE SEVENTH

1. A chord of the seventh makes available three inversions in contrast to the two inversions of a triad. (cf. Chapters IV and VI.) Thus, in the matter of variety of inversion effects chords of the seventh offer composers vastly more material with which to work, which can be stated arithmetically as follows:

> 4 kinds of triads
> x 2 inversions
> ___
> 8 inversion effects

> 7 kinds of chords of the seventh
> x 3 inversions
> ___
> 21 inversion effects

Thus, the combinatorial availabilities are increased enormously.

2. A chord of the seventh and its three inversions are structured intervalically as follows:

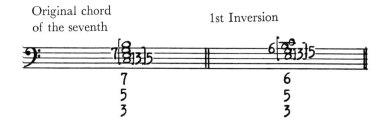

Original chord
of the seventh

1st Inversion

7
5
3

6
5
3

2nd Inversion   3rd Inversion

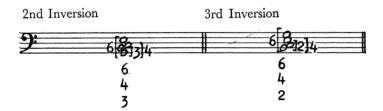

$$\begin{matrix} 6 \\ 4 \\ 3 \end{matrix} \qquad\qquad \begin{matrix} 6 \\ 4 \\ 2 \end{matrix}$$

Unless there is some especially valid reason for using all of the numbers, such as to show chromatic treatment, these chord formations are usually figured simply as 7, $\frac{6}{5}$, $\frac{4}{3}$, $\frac{4}{2}$ or 2 respectively.

3. The resolutions of the inversions of chords of the seventh are carried out according to the instructions given in paragraph 5 of Chapter IX. Items (1) and (3) therein are especially important. Otherwise, no new instructions are necessary. The following quotations are from Bach's 371 Chorales.

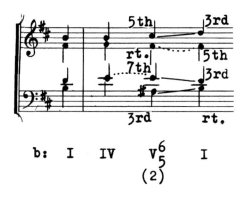

The 7th in the tenor is *prepared* by the root of the preceding IV and resolves stepwise to the 3rd of the I, while the leading-tone in the bass ascends to the root of the I.

102

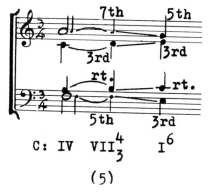

C: IV VII$_3^4$ I^6

(5)

The 7th and 5th of this VII $\frac{4}{3}$ (cf. Chapter IX, paragraph 5(2)), being actually a double passing-note effect, are both "prepared" in the preceding IV triad and resolve downward while the leading-tone, the root, ascends to the root in the I^6. The $\frac{4}{3}$ as a chord, other than as a passing effect, is quite rare.

D: I II^2 V^6 I___

(3)

G: I^6 IV^2 VII^6 I

(1)

In these two examples no leading-tone is involved.

4. From the illustrations provided in paragraph 3, the normal resolutions of inverted chords of the seventh should be clear. The 7th, wherever placed in the chord, is usually prepared in the preceding chord and normally resolves downward. However, one special case does proceed otherwise. In the progression I - V$\frac{4}{3}$ - I^6 the 7th in the V$\frac{4}{3}$ traditionally ascends stepwise to the 5th of the I.

Of course, the above progression is seen more intelligently *not* as a chord, but as a passing-note effect. The V$\frac{4}{3}$ formation is really only incidental.

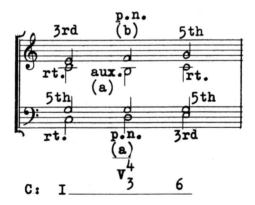

THE II$^6_5$ - V CADENTIAL PROGRESSION

5. The II$^6_5$, in either major or minor, has a special function in preceding the V in a cadence. But is is usually preceded by a I^6 so
arranged that the 7th of the II acts as a 2 - 3 suspension *to* the leading-
tone below the 5th of the V. This is a time honored cadential cliché.

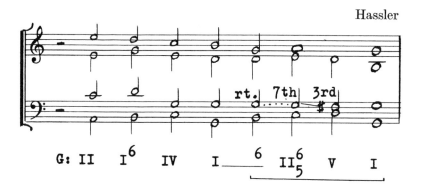

The II$^6_5$ used cadentially but preceded by a root position I.

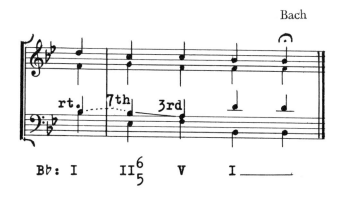

The same cadential progression formula as the preceding but with the
7th of the II $\frac{6}{5}$ in the alto:

Bach

A slightly more elaborate version of the same cadential formula in
which the II $\frac{6}{5}$ is followed by an incomplete II⁷ before progressing to
the V preceding the terminal I:

Bach

6. The II$\frac{6}{5}$ before the cadential V is often used with the bass, that is the 3rd of the original II^7, sharped. This actually produces the V$\frac{6}{5}$ of the V key, and changes the chord of the seventh type from (3) to (2). A typical Bach example follows.

Bach

By this chromaticization a double tonality operates briefly.

7. The II$\frac{6}{5}$ frequently figures in a passing I$\frac{6}{4}$ cliché that originates with the IV^6 thus (cf. Chapter VI, paragraphs 5 - 7.):

See the "general principle" for the correct six-four chord operation as given in paragraph 11 of Chapter VI. A few assorted examples from the Chorale literature follow.

Vulpius

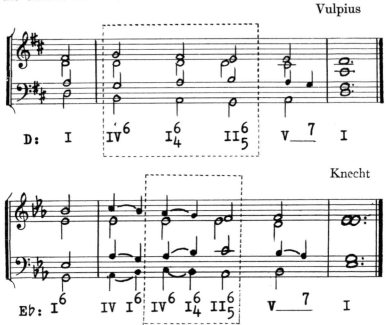

Knecht

17th Century Anonymous

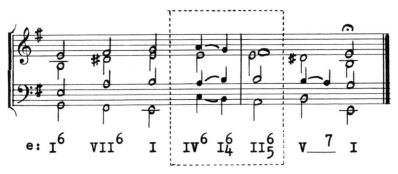

8. While the IV⁶ - I $^6_4$ - II $^6_5$ progression is usually found in the form shown in various rhythmic contexts above, it does not follow that it is never treated with some freedom. Two rather exceptional instances by Bach follow.

INVERSIONS OF THE V⁷

9. The three inversions of the V⁷ all resolve quite naturally to the I triad, and are most often found functioning in this way. Except for the V $^4_3$, when operating as a specific passing effect as is shown in paragraph 4, the usual resolution forms are those given below. These are the same in both major and minor.

rt.   5th   rt.   5th   rt.   5th

7th   3rd   7th   3rd   5th   rt.

5th   rt.   3rd   rt.   3rd   rt.

3rd   rt.   5th   rt.   7th   3rd

$$V^6_5 \quad I \quad V^4_3 \quad I \quad V^2 \quad I^6$$

The three upper notes of each inversion can, of course, be distributed vertically in any of the six arrangements listed in Chapter I, paragraph 5. Also in the case of the $\frac{6}{5}$ and 2 inversions, it is fairly common to let the 5th ascend stepwise to the 3rd of the I triad instead of descending stepwise to the root, especially in minor.

"NON-HARMONIC" HARMONIES

10. From all of the examples that are given up to this point, it can be observed that passing-notes and auxiliary-notes fall into three categories in their relationships to the chords against which they operate:

(1) purely non-harmonic,

C: I_____   I_____ 6

110

(2) raising the dissonance level of the same chord,

(3) bringing about a new chord.

It is through the last of these relationships that six-four chords are formed. And it is through the second and third relationships that most inverted chords of the seventh in conventional harmonization come about. The following Bach quotations will show how such passing harmonic effects may occur.

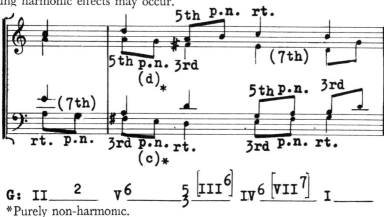

*Purely non-harmonic.

111

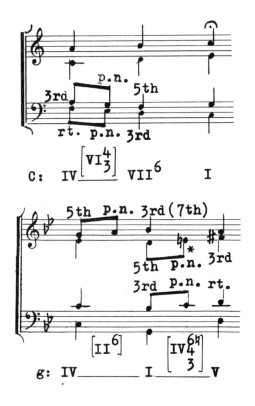

*Melodic minor scale (cf. Chapter IX, paragraph 3 (2)).
In general it will be found that when passing-notes and auxiliary-notes
are permitted to create such chords of the seventh, whatever note becomes the 7th of the "non-harmonic" passing chord usually is resolved
"correctly". (cf. Chapter IX, paragraph 5 (1)).

EXERCISES

Harmonize the following basses. Plan out the doublings within
the harmonies so that the inversions of the chords of the seventh can
be considered either as chords or as passing-note and/or auxiliary-note
formations.

112

113

Chapter XI

CHORDS OF THE NINTH, ELEVENTH AND THIRTEENTH

1. A chord of the ninth is constructed by superimposing a major or minor 3rd upon a chord of the seventh. At first glance it would appear that this process would produce 14 different kinds of chords of the ninth. But this is not so. Two of these superimposed 3rds form an 8ve enharmonically with a member of the chord of the seventh so that in reality only 12 different chords of the ninth are possible. These chords can also be seen as a combination of two chords of the seventh with three common notes. The following list shows in full all possible chords of the ninth.

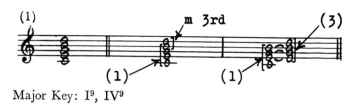

Major Key: I⁹, IV⁹

Minor Key: VI⁹

(3) m 3rd (6)

(2) (2)

Minor Key: V⁹

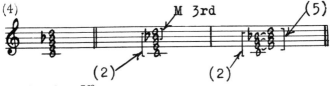

(4) M 3rd (5)

(2) (2)

Major Key: V⁹
Minor Key with raised 6th degree (Melodic Minor Scale):
  IV⁹

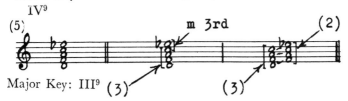

(5) m 3rd (2)

Major Key: III⁹ (3) (3)

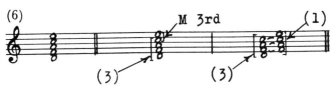

(6) M 3rd (1)

(3) (3)

Major Key: II⁹, VI⁹
Minor Key: IV⁹

(7) m 3rd (7)

(4) (4)

Minor Key: I⁹

115

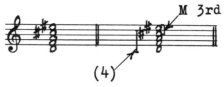

NOT a chord of the ninth as the 9th is an enharmonic 8ve above the 3rd.

(8)

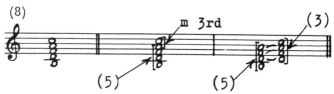

Major Key: VII⁹
Minor Key: II⁹

(9)

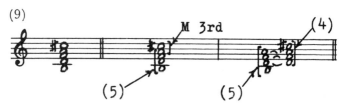

Minor Key with raised 6th degree (Melodic Minor Scale): VI⁹

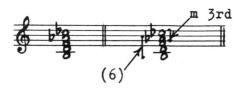

NOT a chord of the ninth as the 9th is an enharmonic 8ve above the root.

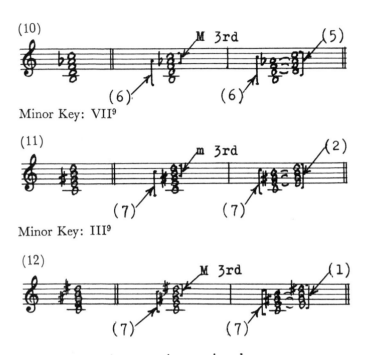

Minor Key: VII⁹

Minor Key: III⁹

Does not occur in any major or minor key.

2. Each chord of the ninth makes available four inversions:

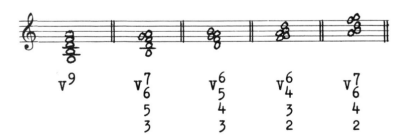

$$\text{V}^9 \qquad \text{V}^7_6 \qquad \text{V}^6_5 \qquad \text{V}^6_4 \qquad \text{V}^7_6$$
$$\qquad\qquad 5 \qquad 4 \qquad 3 \qquad 4$$
$$\qquad\qquad 3 \qquad 3 \qquad 2 \qquad 2$$

3. The principles governing the correct resolution of a chord of the seventh are applicable to chords of the ninth. Referring to paragraph 5 of Chapter IX, when the beginning of item (1) is amended to read "the 7th and 9th should resolve either" etc. these four stated voice-leading principles are quite adequate to meet any resolution problems involving chords of the ninth; or, for that matter, chords of the eleventh and thirteenth. These are discussed later.

4. Because a chord of the ninth consists of five notes, one note must be omitted in four-part harmony. Generally the note to be omitted is one that does not require stepwise resolution either up or down. In the V^9, the chord of the ninth most frequently encountered, the 5th is as a rule omitted. Some theorists contend that the VII^7 is a V^9 minus its root, the latter having no resolution tendencies.

5. Due to the fact that in four-part harmony a chord of the ninth or any of its inversions will have to be incomplete because of the discrepancy between the number of chord members and the number of voices to perform them, a curious situation comes into being that can give rise to some unrealistic analysis. Take for example the following passage by Bach wherein auxiliary-notes (c) and (e) come in the bass and alto of a IV^6.

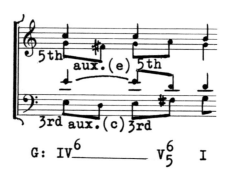

This double auxiliary-note formation is too simple a situation to require further comment. But, should one be inclined to make a more "fussy" analysis, the double auxiliary-notes moving against the root and 3rd of the IV triad produce a correctly resolved V^9 chord with its 5th omitted. This analytical possibility becomes especially clear when the quarter-notes are written as tied eighth-notes as is sometimes done in organ music.

$$\text{G: IV}^6 \quad \text{V}^9 \quad \text{IV}^6 \quad \text{V}^6_5 \quad \text{I}$$

However, it is unlikely that a skilled composer would think in this way. Contrapuntally it is more sophisticated to view it as a simple triad with auxiliary-notes.

6. At this point it seems fitting to inject a parenthetical observation. Harmony being a combinatorial art, it is unrealistic to think of it in terms of *elementary* or *advanced*. It is rather that the student is *elementary* or *advanced* in the way he looks at the harmony. It can be said that one is *advanced* in the inverse of the complexity of his chordal designations. That is to say, that in either creative or analytical identification it is considerably more *advanced* to see a passage as a simple triad embellished by systematically applied discords than it is to think of it in terms of complex chords of the seventh or ninth. This concept is demonstrated in the preceding paragraph and also underlies the presentation of six-four chords in Chapter VI. When, however, chords of the seventh or ninth *do* occur as such they must be treated as pure chords and then *not* as discords within a simpler harmonic framework. But when an analytical option is available, the simpler one is most generally the one to be preferred.

119

7. With the above observations in mind, two analyses of the following Bach passage are given without further comment or explanation.

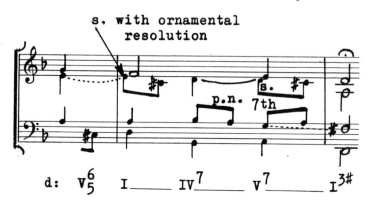

*The V^{11} is treated later in this chapter.

It is unlikely that any composer would think in such cluttered theoretical terms as the second of the above analyses.

8. A bass to feature chords of the ninth as well as chords of the seventh could be constructed as follows,

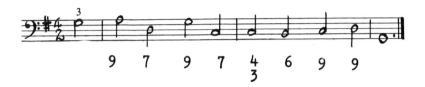

and the harmonization completed thus.

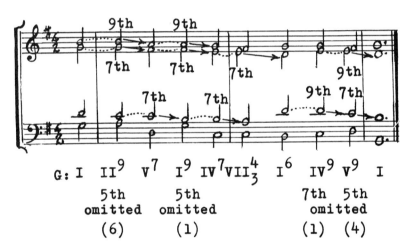

9. The exact duplication of a pattern of two or more chords at a different pitch is known as a *sequence*. This technique is illustrated in the first full measure of the harmonization in paragraph 8, wherein the third and fourth chords are arranged and resolved precisely as the first and second chords. A sequence may be as brief or as extended and as simple or as complex as the composer's designs require.

121

CHORDS OF THE ELEVENTH

10. A *chord of the eleventh* is constructed by superimposing a 3rd atop a chord of the ninth. Theoretically this is possible with any of the 12 chord of the ninth types as shown in paragraph 1. But, generally this intervalic superimposition is confined to V harmony. The V¹¹, built as described above, would appear as follows:

11. A V¹¹ in the form of a suspension in the alto occurs in the penultimate harmony in the second analysis in paragraph 7. As a chord its most common form is that of a IV triad or incomplete II⁷ superimposed over a V bass. The following examples can be considered as typical.

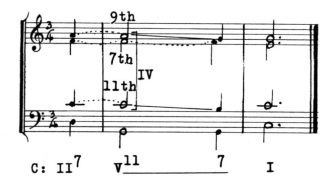

122

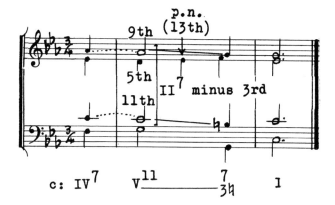

c: IV^7 V^{11} $^7_{3\natural}$ I

This, admittedly, is a very limited view of the chord of the eleventh as a chordal structure and its musical possibilities, but on the basis of what is shown in paragraph 1 concerning the construction of chords of the ninth the student can build and experiment with chords of the eleventh on other degrees of the scale. Such experimentation can include inversions, of which there are five, with the 3rd, 5th, 7th, 9th and 11th respectively, serving as bass.

CHORDS OF THE THIRTEENTH

12. A *chord of the thirteenth* is constructed by superimposing a 3rd atop a chord of the eleventh. All seven notes of the diatonic scale — major or minor — are now systematically programmed vertically by 3rds.

C: V^{13} c: V^{13}

123

13. As in the case of chords of the eleventh (cf. paragraph 10) a chord of the thirteenth can be built upon any scale degree. But, for practical harmonization purposes, this chord assumes characteristic progression features only when it is constructed with the V as root. Since in four-part harmony three of its members must inevitably be omitted, it will generally consist of the root, 13th and two other notes, one of which may or may not be the 3rd (i.e., the leading-tone). The following progressions of the V^{13} to the cadential I triad are typical.

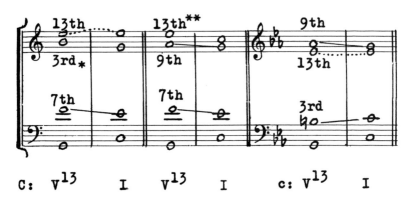

*Cf. Chapter II, paragraph 6.
**The 13th, a 6th (plus an octave) above the root, is not strictly a dissonance and is not subject to the rigid resolution restrictions of the 7th, 9th, 11th downward or by tie and the 3rd upward.
14. Except to reiterate the resolution principles for the 7th, 9th, 11th and for the leading-tone there is not much in the way of theoretical concepts to say about chords of the eleventh and thirteenth. But, the student should experiment widely with these chords on all degrees of the scale in order to become familiar with their sound and to assess their usefulness to him in his creative endeavors. Many harmonic effects of varying shades of dissonance that are not to be found in the traditional musical literature are available and may well prove to be surprisingly successful artistically in particular compositional situations.

124

15. Two simple commonplace triadic chord formations can be seen as incomplete V^{13} chords, namely, the III^6 and I^6_4. The following illustration shows how this happens.

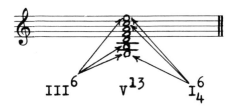

Of course, in the same way and through the same theoretical reasoning any chord of the sixth or six-four could be considered within the larger and dissonant framework; that is, as an incomplete chord of the thirteenth built upon whatever note is in the bass. The same thinking can be applied to any of the seven inversions of a chord of the seventh or ninth (three of the chord of the seventh and four of the chord of the ninth) as they all contain a 6th above the bass. But, such a concept, while being theoretically demonstrable, may well prove to be more cumbersome than creatively helpful.

16. One general structural principle for all chords of the ninth, eleventh and thirteenth must be stressed: *it is customary to keep the 9th above the root and at least a 9th apart.* This restriction tends to make all inversions of these chords unavailable unless the root is omitted, which omission reduces the chord to a lower dissonance level. However, it must be left to the student's discretion whether this time honored restriction is valid at a time when dissonance is employed with far greater freedom than it was when the rule was formulated.

17. Lest it be inferred from what is said above that only V harmony is utilized for the higher dissonance level chords, the following passage is given as a modest illustration of how these chords, when constructed upon other degrees of the scale, may be employed.

A: I   IV¹³   V¹³   VI¹³   VII¹¹III¹¹ V¹³   I

EXERCISES

Harmonize the following basses, bearing in mind all resolution principles given thus far.

CHAPTER XII

MELODY HARMONIZATION WITH CHORDS OF THE SEVENTH, NINTH, ELEVENTH AND THIRTEENTH

1. In order to harmonize a melody with chords of four or more members it must always be determined whether the given melody provides opportunities for the correct preparation and resolution of the dissonant members of the chords should these be in the melodic line. In general there are three thematic features to look for:

(1) repeated or tied (or dotted) notes,

(2) repeated or tied notes or a note descending stepwise,

(3) leading-tone ascending by minor 2nd.

2. Repeated or tied notes can provide the preparation for a 7th, 9th, 11th or 13th and/or the resolution of same to a common note in the next chord.

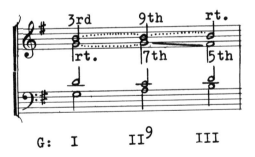

The theoretical problem now arises whether the II⁹ actually is a chord, or whether it is a harmonic illusion resulting from a passing-note and an auxiliary-note striking simultaneously. The latter view becomes strengthened when repeated notes are combined into notes of longer value. (Cf. Chapter XI, paragraph 6-7.)

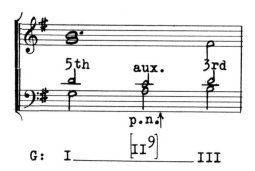

Another treatment of the same repeated notes with three different chords follows. However, in this case the passing discord type of analysis illustrated above is not possible because of the leaps in the bass to and from the second chord.

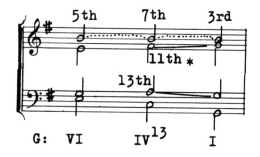

*Leading-tone.

128

3. A note descending stepwise can successfully resolve a 7th, 9th, 11th or 13th should one of these chord members come in the melodic line. (Cf. Chapter XI, paragraph 13, footnote **.)

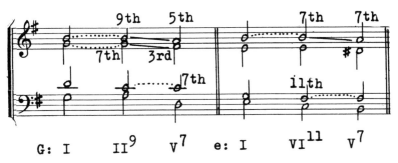

Such a progression is doubly certain when the dissonant element is introduced by a common note in the preceding chord to insure its preparation.

4. When within a melody the leading-tone ascends to the tonic note, some form of the V seventh, ninth, eleventh or thirteenth can be used successfully to harmonize the leading-tone.

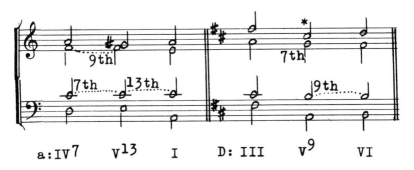

*In the case of V harmony it is unrealistic to insist upon preparation of the dissonant chord members. To the modern ear any form of V harmony is so mildly dissonant that preparation is hardly necessary.

129

5. The suggestions given in paragraphs 2 - 4 above with the material given in Chapters III, V and VII should enable the student to harmonize acceptably and effectively any simple diatonic melody with whatever degree of dissonance may be desired.

6. The following is the Chorale form of a portion of a well known melody by Praetorius.

A harmonization employing dissonant chords might be constructed as follows:

$$I \quad IV^9 \quad III \quad II^{13} \quad VI^6 \quad \overbrace{II^{11} \quad V^{13}}^{} \quad VI$$

$$(III^6\text{-}V)$$

$$IV \quad VI^6_5 \quad VII^7 \quad IV^6 \quad V^9 \quad I$$

*P 5th - d 5th

Such a dissonant harmonization of a traditional Chorale melody may well be open to criticism as being stylistically uncouth and artistically unacceptable on either musical or historical grounds. It is given here, however, purely for purposes of demonstration. It is not a recommended harmonization for practical performance by voices.

EXERCISES

Harmonize the following Chorale melodies using all chords taken up so far. Identify all opportunities for correct usage of dissonant chords and their inversions.

CHAPTER XIII

CHROMATICISM

1. The present chapter and the next one, being about Modulation, should be considered together. In fact, it may be found expedient to study Chapter XIV either before or simultaneously with this chapter which deals with chromaticism apart from modulation.

2. A note can be chromaticized if it comes a major 2nd below or above its subsequent note. If it is a major 2nd below it can be sharped,

and if it is a major 2nd above it can be flatted,

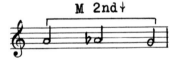

which in either case creates a stronger motion to force it more actively to the next note by bringing it closer to it.

132

3. When a flatted note ascends a major 2nd or when a sharped note descends a major 2nd, the accidental for the intervening note will be a natural.

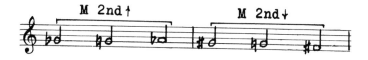

4. When a sharped note ascends a major 2nd or when a flatted note descends a major 2nd, the accidentals will be a double sharp or double flat respectively.

5. It is not uncommon for chromaticized notes to be written enharmonically. For instance, in the preceding illustration the G-double-sharp could be written as A-natural and the A-double-flat as G-natural. This might occur most often in tempered music for the piano or organ where enharmonic notation is inconsequential.

6. No motion is achieved by altering a note that ascends by minor 2nd or descends by a minor 2nd as such chromaticization would merely produce the enharmonic equivalent of the second note.

133

7. By applying accidentals to one or more members of a chord, the nature of the chord can thereby be changed. In triads, one chromatic change can operate in the following ten ways:

(1) *major triads* become *minor* when the 3rd is lowered,

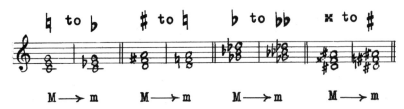

(2) *major triads* become *diminished* when the root is raised,

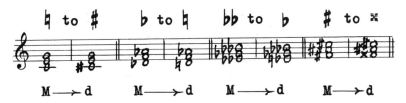

(3) *major triads* become *augmented* when the 5th is raised,

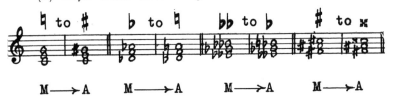

(4) *minor triads* become *major* when the 3rd is raised,

(5) *minor triads* become *augmented* when the root is lowered,

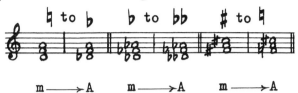

(6) *minor triads* become *diminished* when the 5th is lowered,

(7) *diminished triads* become *major* when the root is lowered,

(8) *diminished triads* become *minor* when the 5th is raised,

(9) *augmented triads* become *minor* when the root is raised,

(10) *augmented triads* become *major* when 5th is lowered.

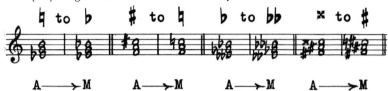

8. Two simultaneous chromaticizations within a triad can produce the following twelve chord transformations:

  (1) *major triads* become *augmented* when the root and 3rd are lowered,

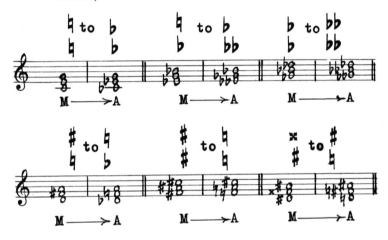

  (2) *major triads* become *diminished* when the 3rd and 5th are lowered,

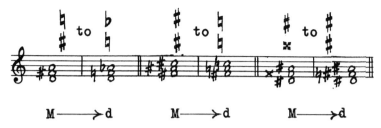

M——→d   M——→d   M——→d

(3) *major triads* become *minor* when the root and 5th are raised,

M——→m   M——→m   M——→m

M——→m   M——→m   M——→m

(4) *minor triads* become *diminished* when the root and 3rd are raised,

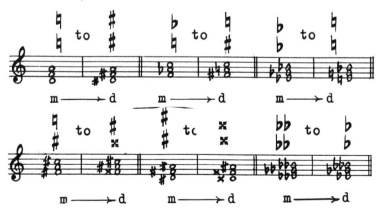

m——→d   m——→d   m——→d

m——→d   m——→d   m——→d

137

(5) *minor triads* become *augmented* when the 3rd and 5th are raised,

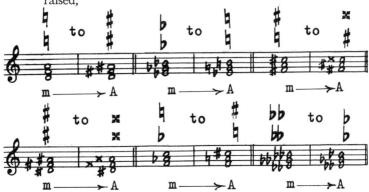

(6) *minor triads* become *major* when the root and 5th are lowered,

(7) *diminished triads* become *minor* when the root and 3rd are lowered,

(8) *diminished triads* become *major when the* 3rd and 5th are raised,

(9) *diminished triads* become *augmented* when the root is lowered and the 5th raised,

(10) *augmented triads* become *major* when the root and 3rd are raised,

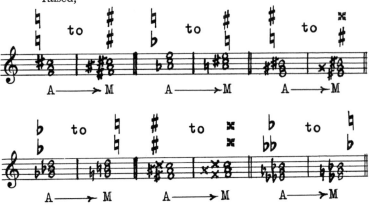

(11) *augmented triads* become *minor* when the 3rd and 5th are lowered,

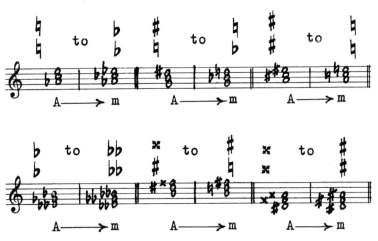

(12) *augmented triads* become *diminished* when the root is raised and the 5th lowered.

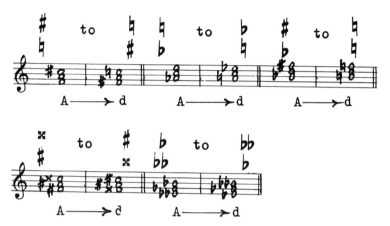

9. Employed as passing-note effects such chromatic changes can bring about a wide variety of interesting harmonic colorings that may or may not suggest new keys along the way. The principle is simply illustrated in this chromatically flowing passage, which never ventures outside the narrow confines of the diatonic triads.

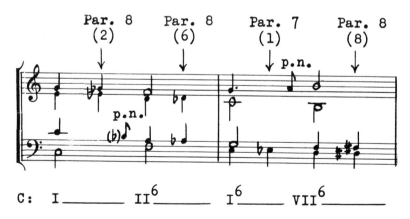

141

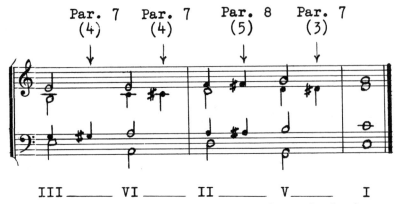

III _____ VI _____ II _____ V _____ I

10. In paragraphs 7 - 8 the accidentals do not change the chord members. That is to say, root remains as root, 3rd as 3rd and 5th as 5th throughout. However, it is possible to chromaticize two notes of a triad so as to produce an entirely different chord enharmonically with a different note as root.

Further experimentation in this direction will yield many effective changes.

11. Chromaticization need not be confined to passing effects. In the following line from a Bach Chorale the III⁶ in the fifth chord with the 3rd sharped in the bass becomes transformed thereby from a minor to a major triad (cf. paragraph 7 (4)) and as such relates to the subsequent chord as V⁶ to I in the key of D minor, the relative minor of F major.

142

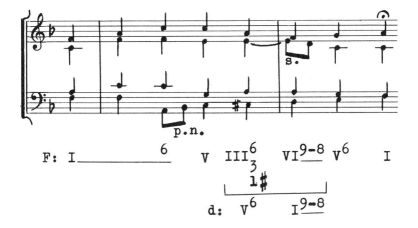

F: I_____ 6   V III$^6_3$ VI$^{9-8}$ v^6 I

1♯

d: v^6 I$^{9-8}$

12. In the above illustration C-natural moves to C-sharp in the same voice, the bass. *Cross relation* occurs when a natural note and the same note chromaticized, or vice versa, come in two contiguous chords in different voices. This is generally better avoided. In fact, cross relation is always included amongst the traditional "errors" in academic harmony. However, it would be unrealistic to say that in practical music even by the greatest composers cross relation is *never* to be encountered. The following instances are from Chorale harmonizations by Bach.

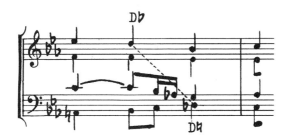

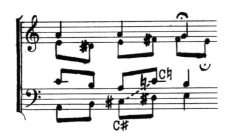

But such cases are exceptions and not the rule. Unless some compelling reason requires the effect of cross relation, it should be avoided.
13. Since a chord of the seventh, ninth, etc. can be seen as two or more triads sounding simultaneously (cf. Chapter IX, paragraphs 2 (3) and 3), the function of accidentals as shown in paragraphs 7 and 8 can be applied readily to these more complex chords. Two especially commonly used chromatic adjustments of chords of the seventh require special identification.

THE V⁷ ON VARIOUS DEGREES OF THE SCALE

14. A V⁷ formation — that is, a type (2) chord of the seventh (cf. Chapter IX, paragraph 3) — can be constructed on various scale degrees by means of the following chromaticizations within other chords of the seventh:

    (1) Type (1) with 7th lowered

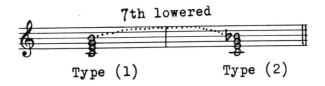

I^7 *in major* becomes V^7 of the major or minor key the I of which is a perfect 4th above the I of the original key.

IV^7 *in major* becomes V^7 of the major or minor key the I of which is a major 2nd below the I of the original key.

VI^7 *in minor* becomes V^7 of the major or minor key the I of which is a minor 2nd above the I of the original key.

(2) Type (3) with 3rd raised

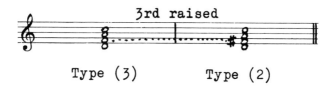

II^7 *in major* becomes V^7 of the major or minor key the I of which is a perfect 5th above the I of the original key.

III^7 *in major* becomes V^7 of the major or minor key the I of which is a minor 3rd below the I of the original key.

IV^7 *in minor* becomes V^7 of the major or minor key the I of which is a major 2nd below the I of the original key.

VI^7 *in major* becomes V^7 of the major or minor key the I of which is a major 2nd above the I of the original key.

(3) Type (4) with the 3rd raised and 7th lowered

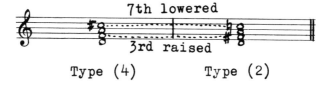

I^7 *in minor* becomes V^7 of the major or minor key the I of which is a perfect 4th above the I of the original key.

(4) Type (5) with the 3rd and 5th raised

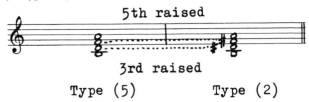

VII^7 *in major* becomes V^7 of the major or minor key the I of which is a major 3rd above the I of the original key.

II^7 *in minor* becomes V^7 of the major or minor key the I of which is a perfect 5th above the I of the original key.

(5) Type (5) with the root and 7th lowered

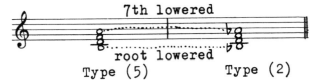

VII^7 *in major* becomes V^7 of the major or minor key the I of which is a minor 3rd above the I of the original key.

II^7 *in minor* becomes V^7 of the major or minor key the I of which is a diminished 5th above the I of the original key.

(6) Type (6) with the root lowered

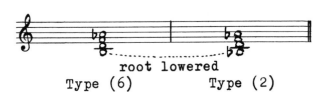

146

VII[7] *in minor* becomes V[7] of the major or minor key the I of which is
a minor 3rd above the I of the original key.

(7) Type (7) with the 5th and 7th lowered

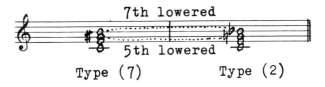

III[7] *in minor* becomes V[7] of the major or minor key the I of which is
a major 3rd below the I of the original key.

15. Such chromatically formed V[7] and their inversions (cf. Chapter
X) are amongst the most commonly used harmonies. The following
is quoted from a Bach Chorale harmonization.

THE DIMINISHED SEVENTH CHORD

16. The second chord of the seventh that is often chromatically contrived on various scale degrees is the Diminished Seventh Chord, which is type (6) shown in paragraph 3 of Chapter IX. It can be formed by applying accidentals in the following ways:

(1) Type (1) with root raised and 7th lowered

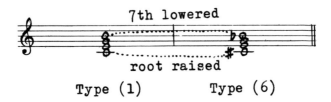

I^7 *in major* becomes VII^7 of the minor key the I of which is a major 2nd above the I of the original key.

IV^7 *in major* becomes VII^7 of the minor key the I of which is a perfect 5th above the I of the original key.

VI^7 *in minor* becomes VII^7 of the minor key the I of which is a major 2nd below the I of the original key.

(2) Type (2) with root raised

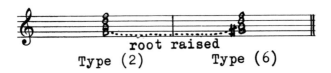

V^7 *in major or minor* becomes VII^7 of the minor key the I of which is a minor 3rd below the I of the original key.

(3) Type (2) with 3rd, 5th, and 7th lowered

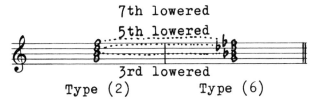

V⁷ *in major or minor* becomes VII⁷ of the minor key the I of which is a major 3rd below the I of the original key.

(4) Type (3) with root and 3rd raised

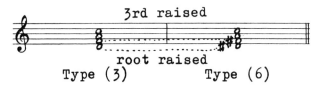

II^7 *in major* becomes VII^7 of the minor key the I of which is a major 3rd above the I of the original key.

III^7 *in major* becomes VII^7 of the minor key the I of which is an augmented 4th above the I of the original key.

IV^7 *in minor* becomes VII^7 of the minor key the I of which is a perfect 5th above the I of the original key.

VI^7 *in major* becomes VII^7 of the minor key the I of which is a minor 2nd below the I of the original key.

(5) Type (3) with 5th and 7th lowered

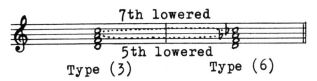

II⁷ *in major* becomes VII⁷ of the minor key the I of which is a minor 3rd above the I of the original key.

III⁷ *in major* becomes VII⁷ of the minor key the I of which is a perfect 4th above the I of the original key.

IV⁷ *in minor* becomes VII⁷ of the minor key the I of which is a diminished 5th above the I of the original key.

VI⁷ *in major* becomes VII⁷ of the minor key the I of which is a major 2nd below the I of the original key.

  (6) Type (5) with 7th lowered

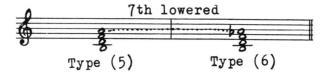

II⁷ *in minor* becomes VII⁷ of the minor key the I of which is a minor 3rd above the I of the original key.

VII⁷ *in major* becomes VII⁷ of the minor key the I of which is the same as the I of the original key.

  (7) Type (5) with root, 3rd, and 5th raised

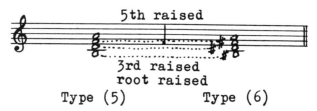

II⁷ *in minor* becomes VII⁷ of the minor key the I of which is a major 3rd above the I of the original key.

VII⁷ *in major* becomes VII⁷ of the minor key the I of which is a minor 2nd enharmonically above the I of the original key.

17. Since types (4) (I⁷ in minor) and (7) III⁷ in minor have two vertically adjacent major 3rds, these two chords are not adaptable for chromaticization into a diminished seventh chord.

18. A pair of Bach quotations will suffice to show how chromatically contrived diminished seventh chords can operate within a practical harmonization.

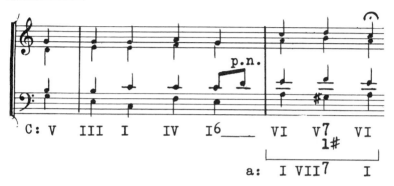

cf. paragraph 16 (2)

cf. paragraph 16 (4)

THE NEAPOLITAN SIXTH CHORD

19. The so-called Neapolitan Sixth Chord is a major triad in its first inversion the root of which is a minor 2nd above the I of the major or minor key within which it operates. In major keys it is contrived by chromaticizing the II triad according to paragraph 8 (6), while in minor keys the II triad is treated according to paragraph 7 (7), the root being lowered thereby.

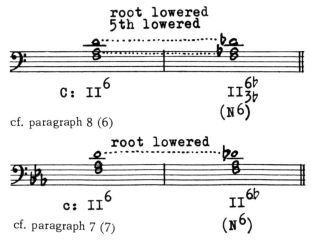

Its traditional function is to precede the cadential V or I $^6_4$.

c: N⁶ I⁶₄ V I

When the II⁶ proceeds directly to some form of V harmony an awkward voice-leading problem comes about in that the root of the N⁶, that is the lowered root of the II, descends by the ungainly interval of a diminished 3rd to the leading-tone (i.e. the 3rd of the V).

C or c: N⁶ V

However, this progression can be made to move more smoothly simply by inserting a passing-note within the diminished 3rd.

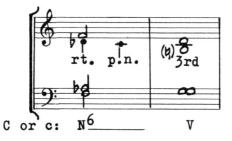

C or c: N⁶ V

This particular voice-leading problem and its obvious solution is exactly the same in both major and minor keys.

20. Other doublings are, of course, possible within the N⁶ so long as inept and clumsy voice-leading is avoided.

THE AUGMENTED SIXTH CHORDS

21. *The Augmented Sixth Chords* serve essentially the same purpose as the Neapolitan Sixth Chord; namely, to precede the cadential V or I$^6_4$. These are derived chromatically from the IV^6 chord. In major keys this is done by means of lowering chromatically the 3rd, which is in the bass, and raising the root.

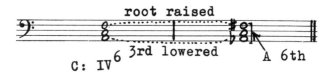

In minor keys only the root need be raised to achieve the same result.

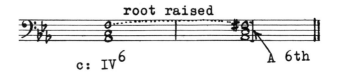

22. In four-part harmony the additional note is supplied in three ways:

the 5th doubled	a note a major 2nd above the 5th and an augmented 4th above bass	a note a minor 3rd above the 5th and a perfect 5th above bass	the same enharmonically

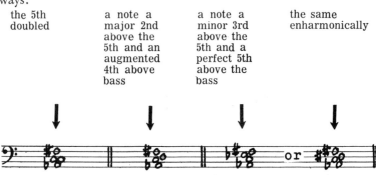

Italian 6th   French 6th   German 6th

154

As indicated above the three forms are sometimes referred to as "Italian", "French" and "German" Sixth Chords respectively. These three chords, along with the V and VII triads, the V⁷ and the N⁶ comprise a set of seven chords that are alike in both major and minor.

23. Although, as shown above, the three forms of the Augmented Sixth Chord are derived from the IV⁶ with or without an added note, the figuration in the case of the French and the enharmonic form of the German chords do not reflect this. In these two chords the note that is the augmented 4th and the doubly augmented 4th respectively becomes the root, at least visually. The figuration is as follows:

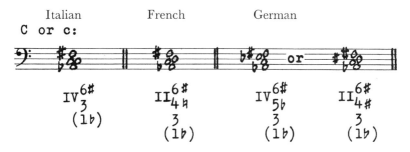

24. In the case of the Augmented Sixth Chords the accidentals in the figuration become a fairly complicated matter. The reason for this lies in the arrangement of major and minor 6ths in the key of C:

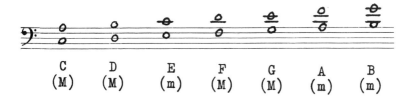

In order to be made augmented the 6ths above C, D, F and G require a sharp, while the 6ths above E, A and B require a double-sharp.

If the lower note is flatted, then the augmented 6th is formed by a natural for the upper note above C-flat, D-flat, F-flat and G-flat and by a sharp for the upper note above E-flat, A-flat and B-flat.

When the lower note is sharped, the upper note of the augmented 6th will be a double-sharp above C-sharp, F-sharp and A-sharp. A double-sharp is not used with the E above G-sharp nor the B above D-sharp, and an augmented 6th cannot be written above E-sharp, A-sharp and B-sharp as this would require a triple-sharp for which there is no sign. These four specifically named intervals would have to be notated enharmonically as minor 7ths.

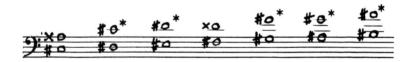

*Minor 7th enharmonic of Augmented 6th.

156

In the case of the augmented 4th in the French Sixth Chord the upper note will be sharped above all natural notes except F above which the B will be natural,

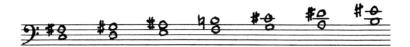

and above all flatted notes the upper note will be natural except above F-flat where the augmented 4th is formed by B-flat,

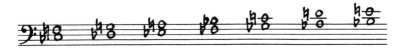

and above all sharped notes the sign for the augmented 4th will be double-sharp except in two cases: B-sharp above F-sharp and F-sharp above B-sharp as the enharmonic of E-double-sharp which is not used.

*Diminished 5th enharmonic of Augmented 4th.

In the German Sixth Chord the perfect 5th is a natural note above all natural notes except B where it requires a sharp, and the enharmonic doubly augmented 4th will be indicated by a double-sharp except above F where it becomes a sharp and B where it would require a double-sharped E which is not used.

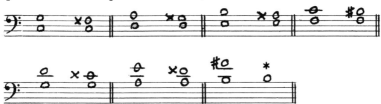

*Double-sharp E as the enharmonic of F-sharp not available.

157

Above flatted notes the perfect 5th is shown by a flat except above B-flat where it is F-natural, and the enharmonic doubly augmented 4th is indicated by a sharp except above F-flat where it is a B-natural.

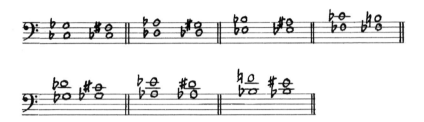

With the lower note sharped all perfect 5ths will require a sharp except above B-sharp where an F-double-sharp is necessary; and it is impossible to notate the enharmonic doubly augmented 4th above any sharped note.

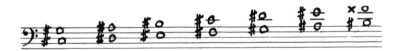

The major 3rd which occurs in all three forms of the Augmented Sixth Chord will be natural above C, F and G, and sharp above the remaining four notes.

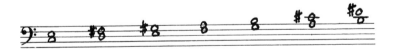

158

When the lower note is flat or sharp, the corresponding accidentals for upper note will be as follows:

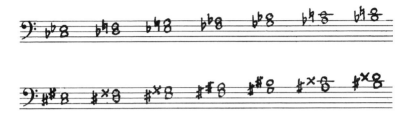

Five double-flatted notes can serve as bass for Augmented Sixth Chords. These and the Augmented Sixth Chords that can be constructed upon them are as follows:

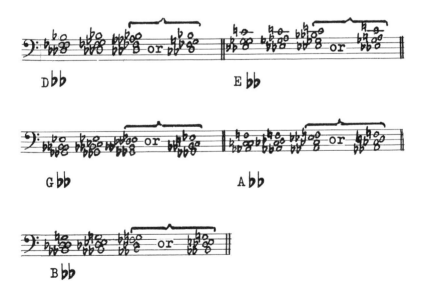

25. The resolution of the Augmented Sixth Chord in all of its three forms lies in the natural expansion by semitones in contrary motion of the augmented 6th to the octave on the dominant.

A 6th   V(I_4^6, III^6)

The two remaining notes normally progress stepwise, by tie, or by leap to their nearest notes in the subsequent chord. The following examples are typical cadential progression clichés.

The above formulas operate in exactly the same way in minor keys.
26. When the German form of the Augmented Sixth Chord progresses directly to the V triad instead of through the I$^6_4$, there comes about an instance of parallel 5ths between the bass and some upper voice that is generally permitted.

To disguise these 5ths one need merely suspend the 5th of the German Augmented Sixth Chord, thereby delaying the 5th of the V triad.

The illustrations in this and the foregoing paragraph treat these three Augmented Sixth Chords routinely. A resourceful and imaginative composer will strive assiduously to devise other and more ingenious voice-leadings together with effective embellishments to meet his artistic requirements.

27. An interesting relationship exists between the Neapolitan Sixth Chord (N⁶) and the German form of the Augmented Sixth Chord. The latter is enharmonically the V^7 of the former. This relationship can be seen from the following diagram.

C: German Sixth = D♭: V^7 C: N^6= D♭: I^6

Thus, in a sense, every major or minor key by means of its Neapolitan Sixth and Augmented Sixth Chords combines with the major key a semitone higher to form what amounts to a double tonality.

28. A typical bass with accidentals to indicate Neapolitan Sixth and Augmented Sixth Chords in various keys could be given as follows:

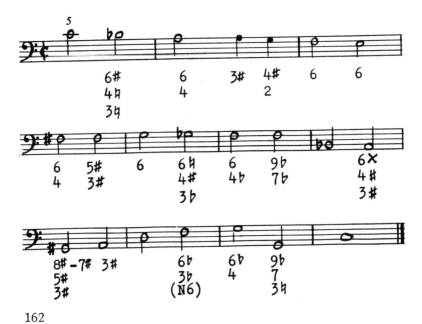

An academically acceptable traditional solution might appear thus:

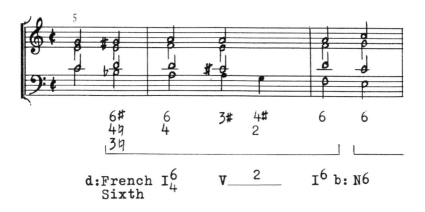

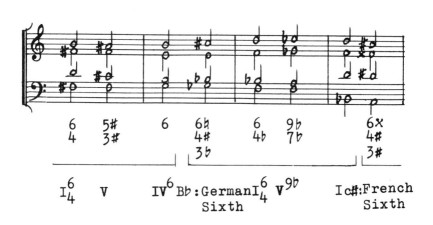

163

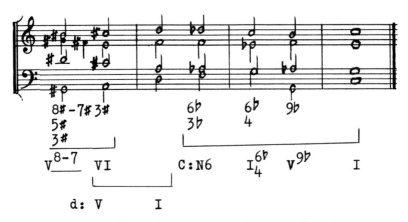

29. The Augmented Sixth Chords are rare in Bach's Chorale harmonizations. Two quotations may be of interest.

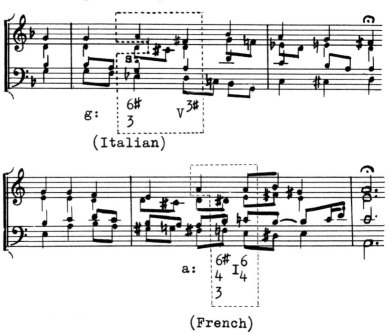

(Italian)

(French)

EXERCISES

Harmonize the following basses, applying accidentals as indicated in the figuration. Identify all chromatically contrived chords according to their function within the key, or keys, to which they belong.

Chapter XIV

MODULATION

1. *Modulation* is the process of passing from one key to another. In Chapter XIII it is demonstrated how a chord can be shifted from one key to another by means of applying accidentals to one or more of the chord members. But, in the strictest sense such chromaticization is not pure modulation.

2. Keys are related to one another in two ways:

    (1) those that have one or more common triads[1], and

    (2) those that have no common triads.

Typical of the first category are the keys of C major and E minor:

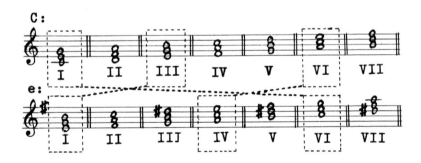

---

[1]A complete listing of all Modulation relationships is given in MODULATION RE-DEFINED by Hugo Norden (Bruce Humphries).

A pair of keys containing no common triads would be C major and E-flat major:

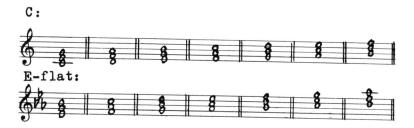

It will be seen at once that no common triads exist in these two keys.
3. An instance of modulation by common chords, often referred to as *pivot chords*, wherein I in A minor equals VI in C major is shown — prematurely, perhaps — in the first of the two Hassler quotations in paragraph 2 of Chapter III. And a case of dual tonality, C major and F major, is given in the anonymous Chorale line in paragraph 2 of Chapter II. In this particular passage the ambiguous tonality results from the absence of the note 'B', either natural or flat, which is the only difference between C major and F major. A simple but effective modulation from E-flat major to C minor is operative in the following harmonization by Bach.

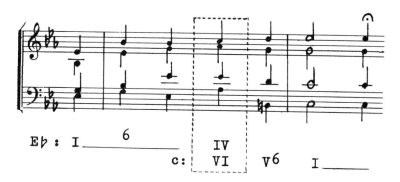

4. The "pivot chord" functions of all triads in both major and minor keys can be tabulated as follows:

Major triads:

I in a major key
IV in a major key
V in a major key
V in a minor key
VI in a minor key
N^6 in a major key
N^6 in a minor key

For example:

I in C major
IV in G major
V in F major
V in F minor
VI in E minor
N^6 in B major
N^6 in B minor

Minor Triads:

I in a minor key
II in a major key
III in a major key
IV in a minor key
VI in a major key

For example:

  I in D minor
  II in C major
  III in B-flat major
  IV in A minor
  VI in F major

Diminished Triads:

  II in a minor key
  VII in a major key
  VII in a minor key

For example:

  II in A minor
  VII in C major
  VII in C minor

Augmented Triads:

  III enharmonically in three minor keys the
  tonics of which are a major 3rd apart.

For example:

From the foregoing system all "pivot chord" modulations can be calculated. In some cases the common chord may appear enharmonically as, for instance, the V in C-sharp minor and IV in E-flat major, but this visual difference does not change the relationship.

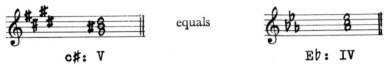

c#: V   equals   Eb: IV

5. See also the various functions of chords of the seventh, types (1), (2), (3) and (5) as given in paragraph 2 of Chapter IX. Types (4), (6) and (7) each appear in only one key and thus are not useful for modulation purposes.

6. A pair of keys having no common triad can invariably be connected by means of a progression in some intermediate key. What these intermediate keys and the progressions within them are can be seen by listing under each triad its other functions. (Cf. paragraph 4.) When the same key is listed beneath a triad in the first key and also beneath a triad in the second key, a modulation through a progression in an intermediate key is automatically established. Thus, the keys of C major and E-flat major (cf. paragraph 2) contain the following intermediate key availabilities.

C major

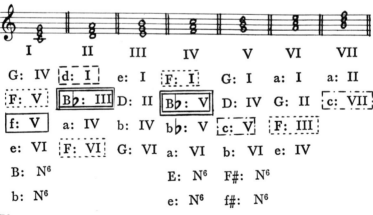

I   II   III   IV   V   VI   VII

G: IV	d: I	e: I	F: I	G: I	a: I	a: II
F: V	Bb: III	D: II	Bb: V	D: IV	G: II	c: VII
f: V	a: IV	b: IV	bb: V	c: V	F: III	
e: VI	F: VI	G: VI	a: VI	b: VI	e: IV	
B: N⁶			E: N⁶	F#: N⁶		
b: N⁶			e: N⁶	f#: N⁶		

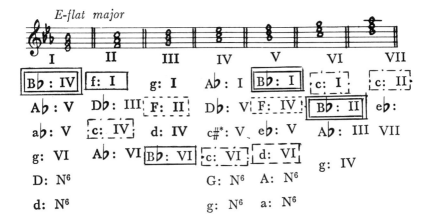

E-flat major

I	II	III	IV	V	VI	VII
Bb: IV	f: I	g: I	Ab: I	Bb: I	c: I	c: II
Ab: V	Db: III	F: II	Db: V	F: IV	Bb: II	eb:
ab: V	c: IV	d: IV	c#*: V	eb: V	Ab: III	VII
g: VI	Ab: VI	Bb: VI	c: VI	d: VI		
					g: IV	
D: N⁶			G: N⁶	A: N⁶		
d: N⁶			g: N⁶	a: N⁶		

*Enharmonic of D-flat minor.

Legend: ⌐F major⌐   ⌐F minor⌐   ⌐D minor⌐
⌐C minor⌐   ⌐B-flat major⌐

7. Common key relationships with N^6 listings beneath the second key are not considered at this time since the function of a Neapolitan Sixth Chord is to *enter* rather than to *leave* a key. This rather stylized progression principle is shown in detail in Chapter XIII (cf. paragraphs 19, 25-26) wherein the conventional resolutions of both the Neapolitan Sixth and Augmented Sixth Chords to the I and V cadential clichés are given.

8. From the tabulation in paragraph 6 it will be seen that the following 25 intermediate key progressions are available between C major and E-flat major:

1. C:I to E-flat:III = F major:V - II
2. C:I to E-flat:V = F major:V - IV
3. C:II to E-flat:III = F major:VI - II (cf. 8. and 11.)
4. C:II to E-flat:V = F major:VI - IV (cf. 9. and 12.)
5. C:IV to E-flat:III = F major:I - II (cf. 15.)
6. C:IV to E-flat:V = F major:I - IV (cf. 16.)

        *   *   *   *   *

7. C:I to E-flat:II = F minor:V - I

        *   *   *   *   *

171

8. C:II to E-flat:III = D minor:I - IV (cf. 3. and 11.)
9. C:II to E-flat:V = D minor:I - VI (cf. 4. and 12.)

      *   *   *   *   *

10. C:II to E-flat:I = B-flat major:III - IV
11. C:II to E-flat:III = B-flat major:III - VI (cf. 3. and 8.)
12. C:II to E-flat:V = B-flat major:III - I (cf. 4. and 9.)
13. C:II to E-flat:VI = B-flat major:III - II
14. C:IV to E-flat:I = B-flat major:V - IV
15. C:IV to E-flat:III = B-flat major:V - VI (cf. 5.)
16. C:IV to E-flat:V = B-flat major:V - I (cf. 6.)
17. C:IV to E-flat:VI = B-flat major:V - II

      *   *   *   *   *

18. C:V to E-flat:II = C minor:V - IV
19. C:V to E-flat:IV = C minor:V - VI
20. C:V to E-flat:VI = C minor:V - I
21. C:V to E-flat:VII = C minor:V - II
22. C:VII to E-flat:II = C minor:VII - IV
23. C:VII to E-flat:IV = C minor:VII - VI
24. C:VII to E-flat:VI = C minor:VII - I
25. C:VII to E-flat:VII = C minor:VII - II

To pick at random a progression from the above list, No. 7 might be worked out thus:

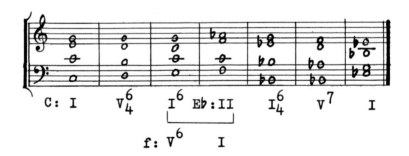

Intermediate key progressions can also be employed to link keys that do have a common chord.

172

EXERCISES

I. Identify the modulations and the pivot chords in the following Chorale harmonizations by Bach.

1.

2.

3.

4.

5.

II. List all intermediate key progressions that could link the following pairs of keys, and compose modulations that utilize same.

  1. E minor - G minor
  2. .A minor - D major
  3. F major - F-sharp minor
  4. B major - E-flat major
  5. G-sharp minor - C minor

CHAPTER XV

MELODY HARMONIZATION IN GENERAL

1. This closing chapter summarizes all that goes before. However, in order to harmonize successfully any given melody a few additional matters must be considered.

EMBELLISHING AND NON-DIRECTIONAL DISCORDS

2. The *appoggiatura* and *échappée* are described in paragraph 5 of Chapter VIII in contrast to the "Connecting or Directional Dissonances" treated in paragraphs 3 and 4 of that chapter. When these occur in a melody they can conceivably confuse the process of harmonizing the melody.

3. The appoggiatura is an accented discord that may be placed a minor 2nd below a chord member or either a minor or major 2nd above a chord member. Take, for example, the note G:

Theoretically, though probably never in actual practical application, this — or any other note — can serve 105 chordal functions but not,

175

obviously, in any single tonality context. These can be tabulated as follows:

> In a triad
> (3 chord members x 4 kinds of triads) .... 12 uses
> In a chord of the seventh
> (4 chord members x 7 kinds of chords of the seventh) .... 28 uses
> In a chord of the ninth
> (5 chord members x 12 kinds of chords of the ninth) .... 60 uses
> In an augmented sixth chord .... 5 uses
>
> 105 uses

Again theoretically, since there are three appoggiaturas available for embellishing this note,

the combinatorial possibilities exclusive of inversions of these chords now is increased to 315. But, it is unlikely for all possibilities to be artistically feasible in one given melodic situation. By including chords of the eleventh and thirteenth as harmonic equipment the functional possibilities increase numerically.

4. When the calculations in paragraph 3 are applied to all twelve notes it follows that the entire triadic system makes available 3780 (315 x 12) melody-harmony situations involving appoggiaturas. And, when the several inversions of the various chords are considered, this number is greatly increased. Hence, if a composer attacked the problem of melody harmonization with a computer oriented approach, he would have available a quite wide variety of harmonic combinations. This possibility merits much serious experimentation.

176

5. An appoggiatura can be purely non-harmonic, as in the case of the one *below* G when this note is the 5th of a triad.

On the other hand, if in the same melody situation the G were the root of a first inversion triad with either the 3rd or 5th doubled, the appoggiatura could be viewed as a member of another chord, in this case the B minor triad.

With the root doubled instead of the 5th, the appoggiatura becomes identifiable as the 7th of a chord of the seventh in the ⁶₅ inversion.

6. In paragraph 11 of Chapter VI it is stated,

> If a six-four chord can be analyzed also as a combination of correctly treated discords operating within a larger harmonic framework, then it can safely be considered as a correctly treated six-four both in structure and operation.

This assumes a new shade of meaning when the appoggiatura *above* a note is applied to the 5th of a triad in its first inversion with the root or 3rd doubled. The following two illustrations demonstrate how this particular situation can come about.

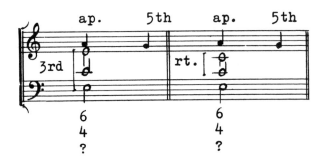

THE ÉCHAPPÉE

7. The échappée is an appoggiatura in reverse. It is an unaccented non-harmonic note *after* the chord member, a major or minor 2nd above or below the latter. The échappée derives its character as a dissonance from the fact that it must invariably be left by leap. The following melodic fragments are rather typical.

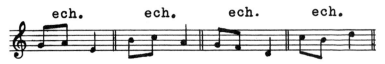

It is immaterial whether the leap from the échappée ascends or descends.

178

8. So long as either the appoggiatura or the échappée is purely non-harmonic, no confusion exists as to which of the two notes is the chord member. But if both notes can be considered as concords an analytically perplexing situation comes into being. To illustrate, the following could be analyzed as a C minor triad with an échappée or as an E minor triad with an appoggiatura, the result being harmonically ambiguous.

CADENCES

9. Five principal cadence formulas are stressed in academic harmony:
  (1) Authentic
  (2) Deceptive
  (3) Plagal
  (4) Half
  (5) Phrygian

Each of these is a chordal progression cliché that "fits" harmonically with specific voice-leadings. These are fully identified in the illustrations to follow.

10. The *Authentic Cadence* consists of the progression V - I. The V
may be built up to include V^7, V^9, V^{11} and V^{13}. In its simplest triadic
form it appears thus:

*When the voice-leading from 3rd to Root is in the soprano, the
cadence is spoken of as being "perfect", with the other two
voice-leadings in the soprano it is generally referred to as "imperfect".

N.B . The only difference between the Authentic Cadence in major
and minor keys is in the voice-leading from 5th to 3rd, which in major
keys is a major 2nd and in minor keys a minor 2nd.
11. In paragraph 6 of Chapter II the Authentic Cadence is shown
with the descending major 2nd in the soprano. The complete voice-
leadings in this cadence move as follows:

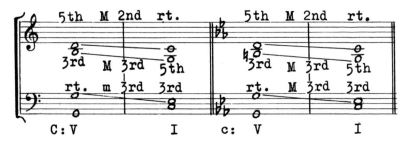

12. The 7th and 9th of the V provide the following additional voice-leadings within the Authentic Cadence.

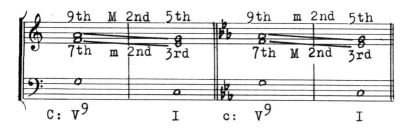

For the voice-leadings in the V^{11} - I progression, see paragraph 14.

13. The *Deceptive Cadence* consists of the progression V - VI and has two forms in major keys and one in minor.

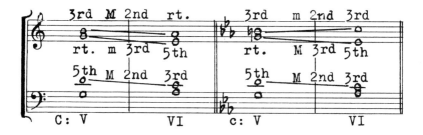

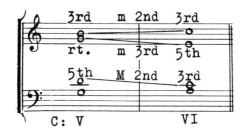

181

The 7th instead of the root in an upper voice of the V descends by minor 2nd to the 5th of the VI in major keys and by major 2nd in minor keys. If the 9th is included in the V chord it will tie to the root of the VI triad.

14. The *Plagal Cadence* consists of the progression IV - I, with voice-leadings as shown below.

The 7th, 9th and 11th of the V being identical with the root, 3rd and 5th of the IV triad (cf. Chapter XI, paragraphs 10 - 11), any or all of the voice-leadings of the Plagal Cadence can be applied to the Authentic Cadence in the progression V^{11} - I. (Cf. paragraph 12.)

15. The *Half Cadence* is a V triad, usually preceded by one of the chords listed in paragraph 18. While in most cases a Half Cadence rests on a V triad in root position, it is not unusual to find a V^7 inversion so used. The following instances are by Bach.

E : I   V____7 VI____ V⁶____ I
                              Ab : V____ IV⁶____ V⁶₅

And, a most unusual Bach harmonization wherein the Half Cadence is on a V⁶:

A: I   IV   VII⁶____ I
         D: V_____ 2____ I⁶₅
                    f#:VI⁶₅_____ V⁶

But, it must be stressed that these three examples are highly unusual.
16. The *Phrygian Cadence* is simply the progression IV - V or IV⁶ - V in a minor key, whichever one successfully avoids parallel 8ves between the bass and soprano. This, too, is a specific form of the Half Cadence.

183

17. Since the three upper voice-leadings of the Authentic, Deceptive, Plagal and Phrygian Cadences can be distributed vertically in any of the six arrangements given in paragraph 5 of Chapter I, the following melodic situations can be identified with specific cadence formulas:

Repeated notes:
 (1) Root to 5th in Authentic Cadence, major or minor key
               (paragraph 10)
 (2) 9th to Root in Deceptive Cadence, major or minor key
               (paragraph 13)
 (3) 5th to Root in Plagal Cadence, major or minor key
               (paragraph 14)

Ascending minor 2nd:
 (1) 3rd to Root in Authentic Cadence, major or minor key
               (paragraph 10)
 (2) 5th to 3rd in Authentic Cadence, minor key
               (paragraph 10)
 (3) 3rd to 3rd in Deceptive Cadence, major or minor key
               (paragraph 13)

Descending minor 2nd:
 (1) 7th to 3rd in Authentic Cadence, major key
               (paragraph 12)
 (2) 9th to 5th in Authentic Cadence, minor key
               (paragraph 12)
 (3) Root to 3rd in Plagal Cadence, major key
               (paragraph 14)
 (4) 3rd to 5th in Plagal Cadence, minor key
               (paragraph 14)
 (5) 3rd to Root in Phrygian Cadence
               (paragraph 16)
 (6) 5th to 3rd in Phrygian Cadence
               (paragraph 16)

Ascending major 2nd:
 (1) 5th to 3rd in Authentic Cadence, major key
               (paragraph 10)
 (2) Root to Root in Phrygian Cadence
               (paragraph 16)

Descending major 2nd:
    (1) 5th to Root in Authentic Cadence, major or minor key
                                  (paragraph 11)
    (2) 7th to 3rd in Authentic Cadence, minor key
                                  (paragraph 12)
    (3) 9th to 5th in Authentic Cadence, major key
                                  (paragraph 12)
    (4) 3rd to Root in Deceptive Cadence, major key
                                  (paragraph 13)
    (5) 5th to 3rd in Deceptive Cadence, major or minor key
                                  (paragraph 13)
    (6) Root to 3rd in Plagal Cadence, minor key
                                  (paragraph 14)
    (7) 3rd to 5th in Plagal Cadence, major key
                                  (paragraph 14)

Descending minor 3rd:
    (1) Root to 3rd in Authentic Cadence, major key
                                  (paragraph 11)
    (2) Root to 5th in Deceptive Cadence, major key
                                  (paragraph 13)
    (3) Root to 5th in Phrygian Cadence
                                  (paragraph 16)

Descending major 3rd:
    (1) Root to 3rd in Authentic Cadence, minor key
                                  (paragraph 11)
    (2) 3rd to 5th in Authentic Cadence, major or minor key
                                  (paragraph 11)
    (3) Root to 5th in Deceptive Cadence, minor key
                                  (paragraph 13)

Any other cadential melody intervals at the end of a phrase or melody would have to be treated according to whatever cadence formula would fit.

18. The V in the Authentic, Half and Deceptive Cadences is often preceded by a I $_4^6$ which, in turn, is quite generally preceded by some

form of IV, II or less often I harmony. This complex cadencing system can be diagrammed as follows:

IV
IV⁶
IV⁷
II
II⁶

II⁷   ⎰ VI (Deceptive Cadence)
                 [I⁶₄] V ⎱ I   (Authentic Cadence)
II⁶₅
II⁷ (V⁷ of the V key)
N⁶
Aug. 6th (3 forms)
I
I⁶

19. What is given in paragraphs 9 - 18 is a fairly complete listing of the more conventional cadences. While it is not totally true that "all is well that ends well", it can be said with some degree of safety that insofar as it involves melody harmonization a harmonization terminated by a successful cadence is generally quite satisfactory musically.

20. Melodies fall into four general classifications for purposes of harmonization technique:

    (1) consisting of chord notes only,

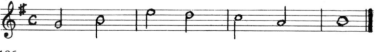

186

which could be harmonized thus:

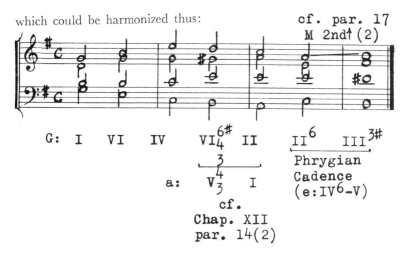

cf. par. 17
M 2nd↑(2)

G: I   VI   IV   VI$_4^{6\#}$ II   II^6 III$^{3\#}$

$\underbrace{\quad \frac{3}{4} \quad}$

a: V$_3^4$ I

Phrygian
Cadence
(e:IV^6-V)

cf.
Chap. XII
par. 14(2)

(2) consisting of chord notes plus discords and other chord notes within the same harmony (cf. Chapter XIII, paragraph 7),

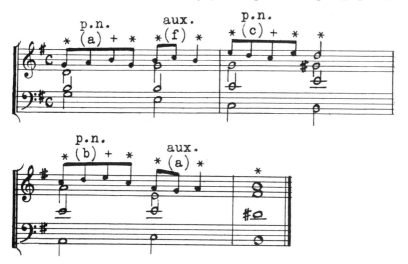

*Notes of original melody as given under (1).
+Other notes of same chord.

(3) consisting of chord notes, directional progression dissonances (cf. Chapter VIII, paragraph 8), and other chord notes within the same harmony (cf. Chapter VIII, paragraph 7),

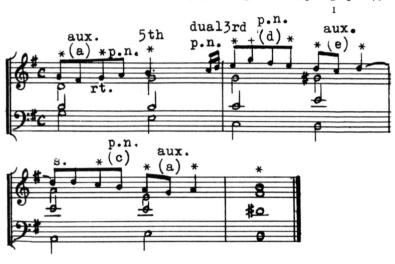

* and + as in (2)
[1]In relation to the upper triad of the chord of the seventh (cf. Chapter IX, paragraph 3 (2)).

(4) consisting of chord notes and embellishing discords (cf. Chapter VIII, paragraph 5 and paragraphs 2 - 8 above) with or without the resources employed in (2) and (3) above.

* and + as in (2) and (3)
[1]Appoggiatura above leaps to the appoggiatura below the chord note.
That is to say, (2), (3) and. (4) are actually variations on (1). It
is usually true that any complex melody is a variation of a simpler one.
Thus, in order to harmonize a melody like (2), (3) or (4) above, the
following order of mental steps may prove helpful:

    (1) establish a suitable cadence (cf. paragraphs 9 - 18 above),
    (2) determine which notes of the melody are discords and which
        are chord notes, and
    (3) harmonize the latter utilizing the principles demonstrated
        in Chapters III, V, VII and XII.

Steps (2) and (3) will also require that it be determined whether the
melody has modulated into other keys along the way (cf. Chapters
XIII and XIV). Brief allusions to keys other than the one in which
the melody as a whole is cast are often referred to as "transient modulations" or "passing modulations" as is the case in the fourth and
fifth chords in (1) above.

21. The presentation of a melody harmonization can usually be made
more interesting by treating the bass and inner voices by

    (1) editings and phrasings, etc., and
    (2) the addition of discords.

The following is a somewhat more musically effective version of (3)

in paragraph 20. The added effects in the lower voice are readily
identifiable.

22. It is generally best, or at least expedient, to ferret out all possible
discords in a given melody so that the harmonization will consist of
the fewest chords necessary. More chords can always be inserted
when this seems artistically advisable.

EXERCISES

Harmonize the following melodies. Experiment with several cadence possibilities to determine which one is the most effective. For the closing cadence, however, it is customary to use either the Authentic or Plagal.

POSTSCRIPT

It would be naive indeed to expect that an imaginative and enterprising composer could abide religiously by the academic rules of harmony. It would be more realistic to expect him to devise ingenious and colorful ways to circumvent and possibly deviate from these rules. A pleasant and informative recreation is to sit down with a work like Bach's 371 Four-Part Chorales and see how many "errors" (?) one can find. However, the knowledgeable composer does not make "errors" willy-nilly, and his reasons for doing so will generally fall into four broad categories:

(1) for some special effect to satisfy an artistic desire,
(2) to incorporate into the harmonization a contrapuntal mechanism such as a canon, palindrome, imitation, fugal fragments, etc.,
(3) to incorporate into the harmonization some symbolic or extra-musical system, and
(4) to divide the time span into some systematically conceived proportion scheme.

INDEX